Discovering Genesis 25–50

THE GUIDEPOSTS HOME BIBLE STUDY PROGRAM

Floyd W. Thatcher   *General Editor*
Robin White Goode   *Associate Editor*
Bob E. Patterson   *Technical Consultant*

Genesis 25–50

Discovering Genesis 25–50   Stephen Stanley
What This Scripture Means to Me   Jackie Stanley
Cover Artist   Ben Wohlberg

DISCOVERING GENESIS 25-50

The Guideposts Home Bible Study Program

GUIDEPOSTS®
Carmel   New York   10512

The photographs on the pages listed below are reproduced by permission of the following photographers:

D.H. Condit: 106 *(top and bottom),* 127, 142
Bruce Cresson: 17, 27 *(top and bottom),* 69 *(top),* 71, 92
William LaSor: 21, 43, 62, 63, 66, 69 *(bottom),* 84

THE GUIDEPOSTS HOME BIBLE STUDY PROGRAM
The First Book of the Bible:
1. DISCOVERING GENESIS 25–50
2. My Working Bible
3. Knowing More About Genesis 25–50

Contents

Publisher's Introduction

Center stage in the drama that covers the events in these eight lessons are three main characters—Isaac, Jacob, and Joseph. They are supported by an enormous cast of actors. We will watch these fascinating main characters and their supporting team move around in central and southern Canaan, in Egypt, and on the road to and from northern Mesopotamia. Even though their language, culture, and geography are foreign to us, again and again we will be able to see ourselves in their thoughts and actions.

The action begins for us somewhere around 1800 B.C. as we attend the funeral of Abraham and then stand aside when his son Isaac becomes the chieftain of the Hebrew family clan. In contrast to his father, Isaac seems a colorless character. Certainly he encountered none of the dramatic incidents that had characterized Abraham's life. For the most part his life was peaceful, without either peaks or valleys—almost, one could say, a mediocre life. Yet it is clear that he was God's choice to be a patriarchal participant in the beginning of the Hebrew race. The promise God had made his father Abraham was renewed

Isaac

with Isaac. God was with him, and that's what counted.

In Isaac we see ourselves, for most of us aren't spectacular leaders but dogged followers. Like Isaac, we stumble along, and if we get press notices at all, they are printed at the end of the classified section. But even as we see ourselves in this picture, we take comfort in knowing that God is with us even in our obscurity. God is the God of Isaac as well as Abraham.

Jacob

The life of Jacob, the third of the Patriarchs, comes through in vivid contrast to his father. At times it is a frightening experience to walk in Jacob's sandals, because we get the uncomfortable feeling that we are seeing ourselves as we watch him lie and cheat to get what he wants. *And what he wants is only what is good for him!* Jacob is an intensely modern man—he portrays in living color the idea that the end justifies the means and expediency has the upper hand.

But in the second half of Jacob's life, he meets God on the banks of the Jabbok River, and while he remains intensely human, from then on his priorities and commitments are changed.

In Isaac, God's grace worked through an ordinary and colorless man. But in Jacob, we see God working through a strong-willed, anything-goes manipulator—an all-or-nothing kind of man who in midlife wrestled with God and carried a scar from the scrap for the rest of his life.

In Jacob, we first see ourselves *but for the grace of God;* then in the last of his life we see ourselves *under the grace of God.* We look in the mirror at Jacob's image and exclaim in wonder, "It's me!" And how wonderful that God also calls Himself the God of Jacob.

Joseph

In the first part of the Joseph saga, we may again become uncomfortable, seeing a reflection of ourselves. This third leading actor in the biblical story is spoiled, egotistical, and tasteless—the original member of the me-first generation. In his own drive for acceptance Joseph is grossly insensitive to the feelings of anyone else.

But somewhere between his hours in the dry well at Dothan listening to his brothers threaten his life, his trip down the caravan road to Egypt as a slave, and the beginnings of his service in Potiphar's house, Joseph did a lot of growing up and maturing, not only physically but spiritually. Next followed his testing years of silence in prison. All of these difficult situations were preparation for the high moments of his life to come when he would be Egypt's second in command.

We may have a harder time seeing ourselves in Joseph in the second half of his life. But here this monumental character becomes a model to inspire us to achieve the greatness God has given us.

From an overbearing, egotistical bore, Joseph emerges into a brother who not only forgives those who sold him into slavery, but provides the means for their comfort and welfare for the rest of their lives. In Joseph, we learn not only how to handle failure, but how to creatively handle success.

As we study these lessons together, I hope we will discover that these three lead characters and their supporting cast were real people who lived and breathed and loved and hurt.

They are us!

But the good news is that God was with them!

He is with us!

He was their God. And He is our God.

Preface

As I began writing these lessons about the Patriarchs in Genesis, our nation was celebrating the 100th birthday of the Statue of Liberty—the majestic lady who dominates New York harbor. On this great occasion we were reminded of the hopes and dreams of many generations of immigrants who came to our shores in search of new beginnings. From those early American patriarchs and matriarchs came a legacy of hope that is so much a part of our great heritage.

Lady Liberty symbolizes our common dream—the dream of making the long journey from all of the things that limit us to a new homeland of fresh starts and new dreams. The journey involves many changes—physical, emotional, and spiritual. Some are carefully planned while others appear to be quite accidental.

This part of our past should help us identify with Abraham, whose life was filled with adventure and whose spiritual history was full of chances and changes as well as hope. We can learn much through our study of the Patriarchs—our spiritual ancestors. Through them, we come to understand that each of life's changes can also be a time of learning and even of new beginnings. As we move in the footsteps of Abraham, Isaac, Jacob, and Joseph, it becomes clear that whatever happens to us—the joys, the crises, the moments of success and failure—can be used by God for our deeper transformation.

As we shall see, Abraham's sons were not always free to choose their times of change. Nor were they able to select those moments of new beginnings. Rather, they had to learn to trust God. Frequently they attempted to gain by their wits and wiles what could only be discovered through faith.

In similar fashion we twentieth-century Christians cannot always choose our times of change and of starting over. But we can learn much by reflecting on the experiences of our spiritual ancestors as we attempt to better understand God's will and purposes for our lives.

Earlier in the Genesis story we saw how God's plan of salvation was not defeated by Adam's sin. We saw, too, how in spite of sin, God acted through such early heroes as Noah and Abraham to insure the movement of His plans for the human race. And while Abraham was not always a role model for good, he believed in God's promises with a vigorous faith.

In writing to the Roman Christians Paul described Abraham this way, "Abraham believed God, and it was counted unto him for righteousness" (Rom. 4:3). It was this faith relationship that Abraham passed along to his children despite their unworthiness. And it is from them that we have received this same inheritance of faith, indelibly inscribed in the Word of God and made flesh in the life of Jesus Christ.

In these lessons we will move from the death of Abraham up to the birth of the Hebrew nation in the Exodus. We begin with Abraham's movement from life into death and end with the promise of his family's movement from death into life by God's mighty hand at the Red Sea. This marvelous story is told against the background of a very down-to-earth family—one constantly on the move just as we are. While conditions and culture are drastically different now to what they were in the days of the Patriarchs, we will discover much in common with them.

We live today in constant tension between peril and promise—symbolized so graphically by the struggle of Esau and Jacob in their mother's womb, by Jacob's wrestling with the angel of God, and by Joseph's conflict with his brothers. Through God's grace, as we study, we will come to better understand our own struggles, even as we see the hand of God at work in the lives of all who hear and obey His voice.

Our studies will highlight the truth that God's blessing came to His special people, the Hebrews, through Abraham. But as Christians, we know that God's promised blessing is for all people, and that His promise is fulfilled not merely by a son of Abraham but by the Son of God. This simply means that our study must be constantly saturated with the assurance of our share not in Abraham's legacy of a *land of promise* but in Christ's legacy of *a life of promise* that knows no boundaries of race or time or space.

Our rich legacy in Christ is best expressed for me in the words found in the second verse of my favorite hymn, John Newton's "Amazing Grace." In a few words, Newton expresses this part of our Genesis story—the journey in faith from peril to promise, from seeking our fortune to discovering our faith:

Through many dangers, toils and snares,
  I have already come.
'Twas Grace that brought me safe thus far,
  And Grace will lead me home.

LESSON 1
GENESIS 25:1–27:45

Abraham's Family Tree

Lord, Make me like Abraham—a pilgrim and sojourner, a lover of God, a seeker of the "city with foundations." AMEN.

Our lesson opens with a rather startling statement, "Then again Abraham took a wife, and her name was Keturah" (25:1). We don't know just how long after Isaac's marriage and Sarah's death this event took place. We do know, however, that Abraham lived some thirty-five years after Isaac's marriage to Rebekah (25:7, 20). Virtually nothing is known about this marriage or these years except our Genesis writer tells us that Abraham and Keturah had six sons (25:2). Most certainly this was a further fulfillment of the earlier promise, "And I will make thee exceeding fruitful, and I will make nations of thee, and kings shall come out of thee" (Gen. 17:6).

Little is known directly for sure about the sons that Abraham had by Keturah. Our lesson gives us a clue when we read that Abraham evidently sent them "eastward, unto the east country" (25:6). Later in our biblical story it is likely their descendants are referred to by the writer when he says, "And Sol-

An Obscure Branch of the Family

omon's wisdom excelled the wisdom of *all the children of the east country"* (1 Kings 4:30, italics mine). And in the book of Job these "men of the east" are spoken of as having great wealth (Job 1:3).

At the same time, we have in the listing of these rather obscure sons of Abraham by Keturah another hint of the relationship between the Hebrews and Arabs. It is possible they represent six Arab tribes and places in Arabia. Perhaps the best known of these places is Midian—the land where centuries later Moses found refuge after killing the Egyptian, and where he married a Midianite woman (Ex. 2:15–21).

Perhaps the greatest irony associated with Abraham's and Keturah's sons and descendants—these people of the east—is found in the story of Christ's birth in the Gospel of Matthew. "Now when Jesus was born in Bethlehem of Judaea in the days of Herod the king, behold, there came *wise men from the east* to Jerusalem" (Matthew 2:1, italics mine).

We don't know for sure, of course, but it doesn't seem particularly farfetched to connect the Magi from the east who brought gifts to Jesus with those ancient sons of Keturah who were sent away "unto the east country" by their father Abraham. And it was to them our Genesis writer says that "Abraham gave gifts" (25:6). We see from this that people of all nations, including Arabs and Jews, assume the position of sons and daughters of God through Jesus Christ. Another favorite hymn of mine (by John Oxenham) expresses this vividly:

> In Christ there is no east or west
> In Him no north or south . . .

The Death of Abraham

Following the brief mention of Abraham's marriage to Keturah and their six sons, our Genesis writer tells us that "Abraham gave up the ghost, and died in a good old age, an old man, and full of years; and was gathered to his people" at the age of 175 (25:7–8). And next we have a touching scene, "And his sons Isaac and Ishmael buried him in the cave of Machpelah, in the field of Ephron the son of Zohar the Hittite, which is before Mamre" (25:9). Once again Abraham and his beloved wife Sarah were side by side. Theirs had been a good life and a long one, and now their son Isaac and Abraham's son by Hagar shed their differences and came together to bury the aged Patriarch.

Family ties are strong—at least, ideally they should be. Recently, while I was visiting in the hospital I met an elderly gentleman whose name was Potts—which was my grandmother's maiden name. Since I've never run into many people by that name, I was naturally curious as to whether we might be even distantly related. My newfound friend was also

The impressive mosque pictured here is located in Hebron over the traditional site of Abraham's tomb. It was here, high in the Judean hills halfway between Jerusalem and Beersheba, that Abraham purchased the field and the cave of Machpelah from Ephron as a burial place for his family. Modern Hebron is a city of approximately 18,000 people, most of whom are Palestinian Arabs.

intrigued by the idea. Since then, we've followed up on every lead we could find, but there just doesn't seem to be a link of any kind. By now, though, we've decided it doesn't matter, because the emerging friendship has formed a bond between us that is just as strong as if we were distantly related.

But for these two half brothers it was the common bond of family that brought them together at the death of their father. Their obvious differences had apparently been set aside in this moment of grief. They knew from experience the truth of the epitaph recorded by the Genesis writer: Abraham "died in a *good old age . . . and full of years*" (25:8, italics mine). This wording reflects the Hebrew understanding of "the good life"—the old Patriarch had lived to see God's promise of heirs fulfilled, and he had died in peace. I cannot help but see a parallel here between the experiences of Abraham and the old man Simeon in the Gospel story. He, too, had lived a long and good life and had waited expectantly for the fulfillment of God's promise to him. When finally he saw the baby Jesus, he could say, "Lord, now lettest thou thy servant depart in peace, according to thy word: For mine eyes have seen thy salvation" (Luke 2: 29–30).

This story of Isaac and Ishmael also reminds me that even a funeral can be a time of healing and reconciliation within divided families. Recently, I conducted a graveside service for a man whose children were at odds. Some of them had not even spoken to each other for a long time. Some were deeply religious while others were completely indifferent to spiritual values.

The sharpness of feeling among the surviving children concerned me a great deal, and I was hesitant when the youngest son approached me at the graveside and asked to say a few words. But my uneasiness disappeared completely with his first words: "We are all children of one father. Let us take this opportunity to acknowledge the hurts of the past and to bury them here as we bury Daddy." As I looked around the family group, I saw tears on many faces. For all, this was a difficult time of loss and separation. But because of God's tender touch through the words of the young son, it became a time of new beginnings.

And so, with the help of two half brothers, Abraham was laid to rest beside his wife in the cave of Machpelah. Incidently, to the curious traveler this cave can be visited today. It is covered by a mosque and surrounded by a town called Al Khalil, which means "the friend."

Isaac Receives God's Blessing

The writer of our story next tells us, "And it came to pass after the death of Abraham, that God blessed his son Isaac; and Isaac dwelt by the well Lahai-roi" (25:11). God had blessed Abraham during his long, productive and faith-filled life. But with his death God now moves the covenant relationship on to Isaac. It would be through Isaac that God's plan for His people would be carried on.

Ishmael and His Descendants

To avoid any gaps in the story, our writer now carefully lists the descendants of Abraham's son Ishmael. As with the sons of Abraham and Keturah, we know little about Ishmael's children. We know that in obedience to God's instructions Ishmael was circumcised by his father at the age of thirteen (17:23–25). We also know that God had promised to make of Ishmael "a great nation" and that God was with him (21:18, 20).

Now, in this part of our lesson (25:12–18) we have "the names of the sons of Ishmael" and we are told next that he lived a long life—137 years—and died a peaceful death among his own people.

As for Ishmael's descendants, the Ishmaelites, secular history has little or nothing to say about them. According to the biblical story Esau selected his wife from among the Ishmaelites. Later in our story we will see that it was to Ishmaelite traders that Joseph's brothers sold him (37:25–28). Then, before disappearing completely they turn up briefly in the Gideon story (Judg. 8:24).

Isaac and His Descendants

Now, though, the Genesis writer moves us back into the mainstream of events, and we pick up again from where we left off in Chapter 24 with the marriage of Isaac and Rebekah (25:20–21). As with

Isaac's mother Sarah, we are told that Rebekah was not able to have children. But in response to Isaac's prayer her condition was reversed by the Lord and "Rebekah his wife conceived."

The Birth of Jacob and Esau

In rather colorful language the writer tells us that it was a difficult pregnancy—"the children struggled together within her" (25:22). In her discomfort and pain Rebekah asks the Lord, "Why?" And in response, the Lord makes this strange statement and prediction, "Two nations are in thy womb, and two manner of people shall be separated from thy bowels; and the one people shall be stronger than the other people; and the elder shall serve the younger" (25:23).

When it came time for the birth of the twins, the first "came out red, all over like a hairy garment" and was named Esau, which comes from a word meaning

A Bedouin tent in the Negev. There has been little change in the appearance of such camps since the time of Isaac.

"rough to the touch." Then the second twin was born holding "on Esau's heel; and his name was called Jacob" which means "heel-catcher," and therefore "supplanter" (25:25–26).

As we learn more about the future of these two babies, we can better understand the Lord's words to Rebekah about the tension between the brothers and the two nations. Esau became the father of the Edomites (the name Edom means "red"), the people who settled to the south of the Dead Sea in the region of Mount Seir. Jacob later became known as Israel. The rivalry was keen between these two nations, but they were always aware of their kinship.

Time has passed and the scene shifts. The twins have grown up, and the contrast between the two is vividly presented, setting the stage for conflict. Esau was an outdoorsman and a hunter. Jacob was "a plain man, dwelling in tents" (25:27). They represented two rival ways of life—the roving hunter and the settled down herdsman-farmer. Then they were victimized by the flagrant preferences of their father and mother. Esau was the favorite of his father Isaac, while Jacob was his mother's favorite. To say to a child, "Why can't you be like your brother?" or, "You're acting just like your sister!" is to fire sparks of resentment that can scar lives for a lifetime.

As parents, we dare not be partial to one child over another. Paul, in writing to Timothy, made it clear that we are to avoid showing partiality under any circumstance (1 Tim. 5:21).

The Stage Is Set for Conflict

We come now to what for us is a strange scene, and yet from other Near East records it would appear that such an occurrence might not have been all that unusual during those ancient times.

First, we see Jacob on center stage—cooking, boiling a mess of red broth or stew. Next Esau enters the scene. He has apparently been out in the country for several days and "he was faint"—famished. The Hebrew word means more than "hungry." It means to be exhausted. Esau himself described it as being "at the point to die"—on the road to death (20:32).

Present Gifts or Future Promise?

You've heard people say, "I'll just die if I don't get it." That expresses Esau's feelings as he sees and smells the broth his brother is cooking.

In the blunt fashion of a rugged outdoorsman Esau gets straight to the point, "Feed me, I pray thee, with that same red pottage; for I am faint" (25:30). Seemingly without any show of hesitation comes Jacob's response, "Sell me this day thy birthright" (25:31).

In ancient times the birthright belonged to the oldest son. It granted him the right to be head of the family and guaranteed a double portion of the inheritance. It also had a spiritual significance. The one who had the birthright inherited God's blessing to Abraham and would become the spiritual leader of the family or clan.

There has been speculation that Rebekah, out of her jealous love for Jacob, may have at some time anticipated this moment and had schooled her son on how to respond. Much also has been written about Jacob's devious and scheming nature as a young man. One thing we know for sure, though, was that this was his moment and he took full advantage of it. Esau, the firstborn son, had something Jacob wanted desperately—the birthright and the blessing.

Esau also wanted something desperately—food. He decided that his present need—great exhaustion to the point of death—was greater than his future position. He surrendered his birthright to his brother and sealed the transaction with an oath. And our writer then concludes the story: "Then Jacob gave Esau bread and pottage of lentiles; and he did eat and drink, and rose up, and went his way: thus Esau despised his birthright [considered it to have no value]" (25:34).

Certainly, one point to this ancient story is the way in which Esau was so ready to sacrifice his future for present needs and desires. Some have suggested that the soup represents our material lives and the birthright is symbolic of our spiritual lives. To follow this thought further we might then say that Esau represents our craving for material comforts and gains in the present that may lead us to sacrifice our spiritual growth in the future. This seems to tie in with Esau's description by the writer of Hebrews—a "profane person." He was a man who was indifferent to the plan and will of God, and so lost the blessing (Heb. 12:15–19).

It is dreadfully easy for us to be critical of Esau, and yet we ask ourselves, "How often have I given in to the expediency of the moment without considering future consequences?" Esau's "live for today" philosophy has a familiar twentieth-century sound. The lesson is clear. None of us can know the future, but we should never be afraid to trust our unknown future to a known God.

Isaac's Story

As our Genesis story moves along, the action shifts from Jacob and Esau back to their father, Isaac. Here we see him confronted with a crisis. There is a famine in the southern part of Canaan, and we're told that Isaac, who normally lived the life of a nomad, moved into or near by the city of Gerar, in Philistine country along the southwestern coast. Its location is thought to be some fifteen miles from what we know as the Gaza Strip, in the Negev desert; Abraham lived there for a time after the destruction of Sodom (20:1). Today this area is a haven for refugees, but in Isaac's time it was a royal city.

While we don't know for sure, it may have been on Isaac's mind to do as his father Abraham had done at such a time years before and move on down south into the Nile delta of Egypt. But the Genesis writer tells us that the Lord had something entirely different in mind and told Isaac, "Go not down into Egypt" (26:2).

Then came specific instructions from the Lord. Isaac and his family were to stay in Gerar where Abimelech was the ruler. And with those instructions came a promise from the Lord, "I will be with thee, and will bless thee" (26:3).

In Gerar God reaffirmed the covenant He had made with Abraham by assuring Isaac that his descendants would "multiply as the stars of heaven" (26:3–5). There's a reassuring truth for us here. Just as God met Isaac where he was, God meets us today where we are—whether in the bustle of the city or the solitude of a desert place. He is with us in the office, the school room, or on a crowded street.

Like Father, Like Son

You will remember earlier in our study that when Abraham was at Gerar, he introduced Sarah as his sister (20:2). Now a generation later Isaac tries to pull off the same charade with Rebekah (26:7). Even though Isaac had just received those startling promises and reassurances from the Lord, he follows the same pattern of deceit as his father had. "And the men of the place [Gerar] asked him of his wife; and he said, She is my sister: for he feared to say, She is my wife; lest, said he, the men of the place should kill me for Rebekah; because she was fair [very beautiful] to look upon" (26:7).

When the ruse was discovered (26:8), King Abimelech rightly pointed out that not only had Isaac sinned because of his deceit but others could very well also have sinned (26:10). Actually, Abimelech was very astute in his observation. So often the deceit of a small minority causes the majority to suffer. For example, it is true that most people are not shoplifters. But because of those who are, stores are obliged to charge higher prices in anticipation of their losses caused by the few.

God Keeps His Promise

Once again we see in this story the marvelous patience and grace of God. In spite of Isaac's weakness and sin, God kept His part of the bargain, "Then Isaac sowed in that land, and received in the same year an hundredfold: *and the Lord blessed him"* (italics mine). In fact, we read that he became very powerful and owned large herds of cattle and sheep. Actually, Isaac became so rich that his neighbors, the Philistines, were jealous (26:12–14).

It is interesting, isn't it, how hard it is for most of us to accept someone else's prosperity. Envy eats at us like a cancer if our friends and neighbors seem to be getting the better of us with their bigger cars and prestigious club memberships. Then if we can't keep up, we become critical and try to put them down in any way we can.

Yes, the Lord blessed Isaac with bumper crops and

great wealth in line with His plan for him at that moment. But we need to remember that abundance and wealth are not signs of worthiness any more than poverty is a sign of unworthiness. One of the great late twentieth-century heresies promoted by a vocal few is that God will pay off righteousness by insuring material gain.

Isaac Is Forced Out

We next see that the feelings became so bitter between Isaac and his neighbors in Gerar that Abimelech resorted to the only option he knew: "Go from us; for thou art much mightier than we" (26:16). International relations haven't changed much in four thousand years. Today we still back up our suspicions and name-calling by saying in so many words, "Go from us."

Isaac didn't retaliate. He moved away from the city into the hilly desert countryside, taking his vast herds with him. Water in this part of the Negev is at a premium, so he immediately tried to reclaim the wells his father Abraham had dug so many years before. His first two attempts to find water at Esek (contention) and Sitnah (enmity) caused nothing but trouble because of the rival herdsman from Gerar (26:19–21).

Room to Grow

Thwarted in his first attempts to find water and peace, Isaac and his clan moved on to a more distant spot where they were able to dig another well in peace. Significantly, Isaac named this spot Rehoboth, which means "Now the Lord hath made room for us" (26:22), or to put it another way, "Now the Lord has given us room to grow."

These words touch a deep need inside most of us. We all need room to be ourselves; we need spaces in which to fulfill our own hopes and dreams. For several years now my adopted home has been in Texas—a place with lots of room. Texas is the "land of the big sky," of wide open places. I have come to see it also as a place that gives me lots of room to be myself and the opportunity to pioneer new ideas and new ways of doing things. The "spirit of Texas" is in the heart as well as in the land. We all need our

"Rehoboths"—not merely as geographical places but as spiritual places where God gives us room to grow.

Peace in Beersheba

Our storyteller doesn't tell us how long Isaac and his family stayed at Rehoboth, but we next find them moving on north to Beersheba on the southern border of what we know as Palestine. It was here that Hagar came when Abraham sent her away (21:14). And it was here that Abraham later made a covenant of peace with Abimelech (21:22–33).

This ancient site has been significant as a watering place over the centuries. And it continues to be a bustling community even today because of the availability of water for irrigation.

Beersheba was to be a special place for Isaac because upon his arrival God spoke to him and said, "I am the God of Abraham thy father: fear not, for I am with thee, and will bless thee, and multiply thy seed for my servant's Abraham's sake" (26:24). What a thrilling experience this had to be for Isaac! The God who talked with Isaac here identified Himself as the God of Isaac's father. God was—and is—a personal God, one who promises Isaac, *"I am with thee"* (italics mine).

This is the great Good News in this part of our story. For all his faults, Abraham had been a great man of faith, a friend of God. Yes, God was certainly with Abraham. But now God promises to be with Isaac as well, a man whom no one ever accused of greatness. In terms of his own time Isaac, though wealthy, was an ordinary man. He certainly didn't have his father's drive and energy. Nor was he ever called "God's friend." Yet God calls Himself "the God of Isaac," as well as of Abraham, and promises to be with Isaac. God is with ordinary folks—like most of us. He goes with us, as our faith is centered in Him.

An Altar and a Well

Isaac's response to this message from the Lord was immediate—he built an altar, a place of worship "and called upon the name of the Lord" (26:25). For the time, at least, his priorities were straight. He had just arrived at what was to be his new home. Obvi-

A girl and her flock at Beersheba. It was at Beersheba on Canaan's southern border that Isaac received the assurance that God would be with him and would bless him.

A well at Beersheba. One of the oldest communities in Canaan, this area has been an important watering place for many centuries. It was here the Genesis writer says that Isaac built an altar and dug a well.

ously, there was lots to do, but he stopped, established a place of worship, and then spent time with the Lord. Here Isaac is a model for us. So often we think we're too busy for a time of quiet and worship. We neglect the refreshment that comes from prayer and the study of God's Word. But notice, even before Isaac dug a well he built an altar!

Showdown at Beersheba

It is obvious from the wording of our story that Isaac felt he was home and safe. He built an altar; he pitched his tent; he dug a well. Feeling secure, he had settled in for a long time of peace and quiet. But then came three intruders from Gerar: Abimelech, one of his key advisors, and the commanding officer of his army.

Isaac was certain that Abimelech's visit meant trouble. "Wherefore come ye to me, seeing ye hate me, and have sent me away from you?" he asks (26:27). He expected the worst, but he would soon discover that God had planned only good from this encounter. How often this happens—to our spiritual ancestors and to us. Events that seem to promise only bad news become in reality the good news of God's will and plan.

Abimelech's words tell the story. "We saw certainly that the Lord was with thee: . . . Let there now be an oath betwixt us . . . and let us make a covenant with thee" (26:28). Then he spells out the details of the treaty of friendship he proposed. Rather than wanting to hurt Isaac, his words show he was afraid of him—afraid of Isaac's wealth and the size of his company. He was also aware of God's blessing on Isaac (26:29). Isaac agreed to the treaty, and the agreement was sealed with a banquet. As a sign of their reconciliation, they "broke bread together." As Christians we can take this as a picture of the peace, reconciliation, and strength that we receive as we come together around the Table of the Lord.

Reconciliation happens, according to God's plan, when other people see in us the effect of God's forgiving presence. In the Book of Acts, we read that when Peter boldly proclaimed that God had made Jesus Lord of all, those who had been hostile to that message were now "pricked in their heart" (Acts 2:37) and reached out for repentance and renewal. I believe that it was the visibility of God's Spirit both in Peter's life and in Isaac's that opened the door of reconciliation.

This part of our Scripture lesson closes with the brief account of Esau's marriage to two Hittite women—a bitter pill for Isaac and Rebekah to take, though the writer does not go into details (26:34–35). And with this piece of news, the action shifts from Isaac to the two brothers of the next generation.

Here in our next section is a spicy drama of Jacob's trickery played against God's faithfulness in five scenes. I use the word "spicy" because it also describes the meal Jacob served his father when Isaac was tricked into giving Jacob his blessing which would normally have gone to the oldest son.

Scene 1 (27:1–5) opens near the end of Isaac's life. The Genesis writer says that "his eyes were dim." In other words he was now quite blind and unable to recognize people by sight.

Scene 1: Menu for Trouble

Sensing that his death is near (27:2), Isaac calls Esau to his camel hair tent. The time has come for Isaac to give his blessing to his oldest and favorite son. Is he aware, I wonder, of what the Lord told Rebekah, the "elder shall serve the younger" (25:23)? Has he heard that Esau traded his birthright to Jacob for a bowl of soup (25:33)? Our writer gives us no hint. But we are told that Isaac gives Esau instructions to go out and hunt for his favorite wild game and prepare a good meal for him. And after that Isaac promises Esau that he will receive the treasured blessing before his father dies (27:3–4).

We can be sure that Esau remembers that he has given Jacob the rights to that blessing. Yet he follows Isaac's instructions and sets out to hunt for his father's favorite meat before returning to prepare the meal.

Meanwhile, Rebekah has been eavesdropping on Isaac's instructions to Esau. Jacob has always been her favorite son, and she is not about to let Esau receive the family blessing. She isn't content for one moment to let *the Lord* work out things in line with what He has told her earlier, so she decides to take matters into her own hands. She calls Jacob to her tent (27:6) and begins to develop the scheme for the "great deception." Modern day television soap operas can hardly rival the plotting and conniving found in this story as we move into the original account of two brothers fighting for control of the family fortune.

Scene 2: The Plot

Scene 2 (27:6–17) sets the stage for the great deception. Rebekah knows that she can copy Esau's recipe for venison. So she instructs Jacob to go out to their herd and bring in two young goats and bring them to her. It is her plan then to cook the meat and season it exactly the way Esau would (27:8–9). When the feast was ready, Jacob would take it to his father and receive the blessing. Isaac would almost certainly be fooled. I have a friend who was deceived into believing the meat he was being served for Sunday dinner was venison only to discover after enjoying it that he had eaten goat meat.

Jacob immediately protests the scheme. Not because he feels it is wrong, but he is afraid of getting caught (27:11–12). He reminds his mother that his brother is a rugged and hairy man while he is "a smooth man." He could foresee being exposed as a fraud if his father touched him. And if that happened, he was afraid he would receive a curse instead of a blessing.

But Rebekah is a very determined woman and mother. After assuring Jacob that she'll take the consequences for their action, she sends him off to get the young goats. Jacob does as he's told, and his mother prepares the savory meal for old Isaac. To conceal Jacob's identity Rebekah brings out some of Esau's clothes for Jacob to wear. And to further insure the success of the deception, Jacob's hands and arms are covered with the skins of the young goats. This way if Isaac gets suspicious and insists on touching Jacob, Jacob will feel hairy and smell gamey like his hunter brother (27:14–17).

Now the plot has been hatched. Rebekah is convinced that the end justifies the means, and Jacob has gone along with the scheme. All that remains is to carry it out.

At the crucial moment Jacob, dressed in his brother's clothes, his hands and arms covered with hairy goatskin, and carrying the "savoury meat" enters his father's tent with the express purpose of deceiving the old patriarch into giving him the blessing which was intended for his older brother (27:18–29).

In response to Jacob's greeting, "My father," Isaac answers, "Here am I; who art thou, my son?" By identifying himself as "Esau thy first-born," Jacob lies to his father. Then in an effort to shift the old man's attention away from his identity, he goes on to perpetuate the deceit, "I have done according as thou badest me: arise I pray thee, sit and eat of my venison, that thy soul may bless me" (27:19).

Obviously Isaac is not comfortable about what is going on. He may have lost his sight but not his sense of timing, for he wonders how his son has been able to kill the deer and prepare the dinner in such a short time (27:20a).

With his answers, that the Lord had helped him, conniving Jacob is not only lying blatantly, but he is also trying to bring God into his deceptive actions (27:20b).

The answer doesn't satisfy Isaac. He knows there's something wrong about the voice. So Isaac asks Jacob, "Come near, I pray thee, that I may feel thee, my son, whether thou be my very son Esau or not" (27:21). This has to be a tense moment for Jacob. Will his ruse be discovered now in spite of all the careful preparations that had been made?

But Jacob wanted the blessing, so he moved in close. Blind Isaac felt his hairy hands, and evidently was convinced. Still, though, he asked one more time, "Art thou my very son Esau?" And for the third time Jacob lied to his father (27:24).

Oliver Wendell Holmes once remarked, "Sin has many tools, but a lie is the handle that fits them all." Jacob certainly found it true. And with his third lie,

Scene 3: The Betrayal and the Blessing

he was now committed. Even if he had a twinge of conscience, it was too late to turn back.

With this final assurance from Jacob, Isaac settled down and enjoyed the meal. But before giving the all-important blessing Isaac put his son to one more test, "Come near now and kiss me my son." When Jacob did so and Isaac inhaled the familiar scent of Esau, he was convinced. "See, the smell of my son is as the smell of a field which the Lord hath blessed" (27:26–27). Rebekah had planned well. Esau's hunting clothes were the final clincher. Isaac now bestows the blessing—a legally binding will and testament.

For me, there is something about this scene that reminds us of two incidents in the life of our Lord. First, I'm reminded of Peter standing by the fire in the courtyard of the high priest following Jesus' arrest. Three times he is questioned about being one of Jesus' disciples, and each time he lies, and in doing so, he betrays his Lord (Luke 22:54–60). And then there was the scene in the garden where Judas betrayed Jesus with a kiss (Luke 22:47).

Like Jacob, we are frequently tempted to cover up our true selves and live a lie. And if we get away with our deception, we tend to justify our actions until we lose sight of the truth. But God sees us as we are and loves us anyway. God, unlike Isaac, is not fooled by our deceptive actions and the masks we wear. He is always ready to forgive our foolishness and give us His blessing.

Scene 4: The Truth

In the next scene the truth comes out (27:30–40). Esau arrives back in camp with the real venison and has cooked the savory meal he knows his father loves. In anticipation of receiving the blessing Esau hurries to his father's tent and tells him to get up and enjoy the meal (27:31).

Imagine, if you can, what must have gone through Isaac's head at that moment! Totally confused, he asks again, "Who art thou?" And back came the answer, "I am thy son, thy firstborn Esau" (27:32). Note the double identification here—"son" and "firstborn."

These words must have been like arrows through

Isaac's heart. The old Patriarch trembled violently and cried out, "Who? where is he that hath taken venison, and brought it [to] me, and I have eaten of all before thou camest, and have blessed him?" (27:33). Isaac knew something was wrong. He suspected the worst, but the blessing had been given, and it could not be taken back. Once the words of blessing had been spoken, they could not be revoked.

Our words have great power to bless or to curse. Once spoken, they set forces in motion that are often beyond our control. The writer of the book of James cautions us about the ever-present danger of blessing God with one breath and cursing or speaking ill of other people with the next breath (James 3:6–10).

Jacob's deceptive words and the giving of the blessing by Isaac had set events into motion that could never be undone. But we shall see shortly that God always has the last word. We may think for a time that our scheming and conniving has worked, but God's eternal plans and purposes cannot be thwarted.

With the truth out, Esau screams in pain—a pain much worse than the hunger he had felt when he had earlier swapped his birthright for a bowl of soup. Esau now knows there is no blessing for him and his children. The writer of the New Testament Book of Hebrews described Esau this way, "For ye know that how afterward, when he would have inherited the blessing, he was rejected: for he found no place of repentance, though he sought it carefully with tears" (Heb. 12:17).

In vain, Esau pleads for a blessing from his father, but it is too late. Instead, out of the agony of his own soul Isaac speaks prophetically about Esau's future. He tells him his descendants will be subservient to Jacob's descendants but that ultimately they will achieve freedom. This prophesy came true. During the reign of David the nation of Edom, Esau's descendants, were subject to Israelite rule (2 Sam. 8:12–14). But they began to rebel under Solomon (1 Kings 11:14–22, 25), and eventually revolted completely under King Jehoram, around 850 B.C. (2 Kings 8:16–22).

Scene 5: The Bankrupt Family

The fifth and final scene of this drama (27:41–45) is one of conclusion and transition. It brings us from Jacob's crime against his unwitting brother to the final bankruptcy of the whole family and the beginning of its permanent division.

While the family waits for Isaac to die, Esau plots his revenge. When the days of mourning for his father are over, he will kill the brother he has come to hate so much (27:41). But once again Rebekah, the eavesdropper, acts to protect Jacob. Overhearing Esau's threats, she tells Jacob to run for his life and seek refuge with her brother, Laban, in far-off Haran. There he could also find a wife among his own people rather than among the Canaanites where they were living, as Esau had done (27:42–46).

We come to the end of our lesson with Isaac's family torn by bitter feelings of hate. Selfishness, deception, and bitter words spoken are, tragically, often times very much a part of our twentieth-century experience. We find that our reactions are not all that much different from those rugged people we've been studying about who ranged across the southern part of Canaan some 4,000 years ago.

But as we shall see as we move ahead in our Genesis story, the relationship between God and His people is not broken even in the midst of hard and evil times. Genesis carries the promise of "New Beginnings," of the fulfillment of God's plan for His people, of healed relationships.

A lady I know was facing the frightening prospect of major surgery. When I visited her in the hospital, she confessed to being scared. But she also said with a smile, "God is with me, I know, for He has given me a sign."

When I asked her to tell me about God's sign for her, she responded, "Last night my sister called. We haven't spoken to each other for eight years. She said that she was going to have an operation too, and wanted to make up so we could pray for each other!"

This is the promise we have as daughters and sons of God—He is with us. Like Jacob we are haunted by past mistakes. Our struggles and failures frequently press in heavily on us. Like Jacob we so easily lose sight of our true blessing. And we fall victim to damaged and broken relationships.

In time, our spiritual ancestor Jacob would learn that his true birthright was not Abraham's position or fortune; it was his faith. And from Jacob, we can learn to claim our true birthright—a life of faith and meaning in and through Jesus Christ.

Father, Help me to esteem my birthright as Your child. Help me to love and regard You as I should. AMEN.

WHAT THIS SCRIPTURE MEANS TO ME
Genesis 25:1—27:45

During the summer of 1975 I planned a three week vacation in Germany and arranged to stay with a distant relative while sight-seeing in Bavaria. A few days before my scheduled flight, I received a letter from my cousin suggesting that I change my destination from Munich to Cologne. She would meet me at the train station, and we would then take a boat down the Rhine River to her home.

On my departure date, several problems emerged at the airport. Due to mechanical failures and stormy weather, my flight was delayed for eight hours. It was a long and tiring wait. Hunger and fatigue began to suffocate my excitement over the approaching trip. As time passed, I became tired, hot, bored, and very uncomfortable. And I worried about whether my cousin would be able to meet me at the new arrival time very late that night.

Finally, we were cleared to board the aircraft. It was then I learned that our plane wasn't the 747 jet which had been promised. In its place was a much smaller, crowded, and seemingly unstable DC 10. I felt cheated and angry by this change. The trip that was supposed to be pleasant and relaxing ended up being bumpy, noisy, and sleepless.

Once the plane landed it took another hour to get from the airport to the train station in Cologne. So, it was very late by the time I arrived, and only a few people were in the station. Shops, banks, and service areas were closed, and my cousin was nowhere in sight.

Staggering under the weight of my suitcases, I made my way down the long hall to the information area. My hopes brightened when I saw a man at the desk, but then I discovered that he didn't speak any English. Suddenly, the emotions I had experienced in the past twenty-four hours surfaced in a flood of tears. I totally lost control as I slumped down on a suitcase and buried my head in my hands.

In a few moments, I was engulfed by a warm and reassuring embrace. When I looked up, I saw a middle-aged Japanese woman. Her silence indicated that she couldn't communicate with me in English. But the expression in her soothing eyes broke the language barrier and spoke clearly of sympathy, strength, and encouragement.

This incident came to mind when I read the familiar words of our Scripture lesson. I could easily identify with Abraham's, Sarah's, and Isaac's feelings of doubt, fear, and helplessness as they traveled as foreigners in new and different lands. And the sense of rage I felt at having been deceived by an aircraft substitution was probably very similar to the anger Esau experienced when Jacob cheated him out of his birthright.

In many ways we find it hard to identify with our biblical ancestors because of the differences of culture, customs, and geography. But in spite of this, we can identify with their thoughts, feelings, and actions. The universality of human emotions—joy, sorrow, trust, doubt, anger, jealousy, hatred, love, fear, courage, etc.—allow us to bridge the gap between then and now. This helps us enter into history as our stories connect with "The Story" of God's people. And by comparing the past with the present, we can understand why the Bible has been called the Book for all people, in all places, for all time.

LESSON 2
GENESIS 27:46–31:55

Jacob's Years in Haran

Father, Help me to receive all that You have for me in this lesson. Amen.

In our last lesson we left Rebekah planning Jacob's escape from the anger of Esau. The plot called for him to go to Haran and stay in the home of her brother Laban. He would be out of danger, there, staying with family until his brother's anger cooled off and he could safely return home.

But first, Isaac's permission must be gotten for Jacob to leave. Because it would look better to have a "legitimate" reason for Isaac to leave Beersheba, Rebekah complained to Isaac about her daughters-in-law, the Canaanite girls whom Esau had married, much to the consternation and grief of his parents (26:34–35). In the middle of her complaint was the implication that Jacob might soon think of marrying, but to have another Canaanite daughter-in-law was just out of the question (27:46).

In effect, Rebekah tells Isaac, "If Jacob marries beneath him, I'll just die and it will be your fault."

She was concerned, and rightly so, with two things. First, she, along with Isaac, was proud of their

Aramean-Hebrew roots. But as important as it was, racial purity wasn't the only issue at stake; the Canaanite women worshiped pagan gods and didn't share the faith of Abraham and Isaac. It was important to Rebekah and Isaac that Jacob's children worship the God who had made a covenant with both Abraham and Isaac.

Isaac's Instructions and Blessings

In response to Rebekah's urging our Genesis writer now tells us that "Isaac called Jacob, and blessed him, and charged him, and said unto him, Thou shalt not take a wife of the daughters of Canaan" (28:1). The old Patriarch, knowing that Jacob was selected by God to become the heir of His promise to Abraham, instructs the young man not to desert the values of the past by selecting a pagan wife from among their Canaanite neighbors as his brother had done.

The historian in my family was a great uncle who very carefully put together a detailed account of our family history. Included in the document was a letter written in England over three hundred years ago by a father to his son. In giving marriage advice to his son, the father wrote, "When you shall arrive at man's estate [when you grow up], use great caution on the choice of a wife, for as that is well or ill done, so is the whole life likely to be afterwards."

My ancestor's advice to his son was similar to Isaac's instructions to Jacob. He knew that the people we commit ourselves to have the most influence on our future attitudes and actions. Our relationship choices are among the most important we will ever make. And our selection of a husband or a wife or of close friends vitally influences what we are like and what will become. I believe God's plan for such choices was clearly spelled out by Paul when he wrote, "And be not conformed to this world: but be ye transformed by the renewing of your mind, that ye may prove what is that good, and acceptable, and perfect will of God" (Rom. 12:2). Jacob's challenge and ours is to avoid at all costs being conformed to the ways and people of this world.

Next, Isaac gives Jacob clear instructions as to what he is to do, "Arise, go to Padan-aram, to the house of Bethuel thy mother's father; and take thee a wife from thence of the daughters of Laban thy mother's brother" (28:2).

Then, immediately following those instructions Isaac gives Jacob his blessing (28:3–4)—the same promise the young man's grandfather had given his father; his numerous descendants would one day possess the land of Canaan.

Although the promises in Isaac's blessing were all in the future, Jacob's place in Hebrew history was now insured by God's promise. Up to this point Jacob's record for integrity was pretty shaded. Happily, the Old Testament writers were very honest and realistic in giving us the story of our spiritual ancestors. Throughout, we see God at work with and through real people who often failed miserably to measure up to His best. Yet, God's will and purposes were worked out in time through them. And it is this truth that gives us courage in our own pilgrimage of faith. Yes, we fail and fall short, but God's promises are as certain as sunrise and sunset.

The Greatest Blessing

There's another side to God's promise to Jacob that deserves our attention. This was the promise that God would be with him the same way He was with his grandfather Abraham—not just as a giver of gifts but as a faithful Friend (see 2 Chron. 20:7; Jas. 2:23).

In 1986 a terrible drought threatened to ruin the farmers in the southern part of the United States. But farmers in the north banded together and sent tons upon tons of hay to their southern neighbors to feed their cattle. This magnificent gesture of friendship carried many of the southern farmers through the crisis period. In this story we get a faint picture of the kind of friendship in action that God promised Jacob—and us.

Jacob's response to receiving his father's blessing and instruction was immediate, "Jacob obeyed his father and his mother, and was gone to Padan-aram" (28:7).

An Esau Parenthesis

You will recall earlier how saddened Isaac and Rebekah were by Esau's marriage to Judith and Bashemath, two Hittite or Canaanite women. Now, Esau undoubtedly witnessed the scene between his father and brother in which Jacob is being sent to his uncle's clan for a suitable wife. So, it is possible that, in his own way, Esau was trying to make up to his parents for the friction with his Canaanite wives by marrying a cousin—"Mahalath the daughter of Ishmael" (28:9). After all, she was a part of the family, too.

We, of course, have no way of knowing what Esau's motives were, and we don't have a clue to Isaac's and Rebekah's reactions. But if Esau married this time within the "family" to try to regain the blessing and his place as the first and favorite son, he undoubtedly missed the mark. By virtue of his Egyptian mother, Ishmael was certainly out of the direct family line, and as Jacob had intimated (27:33–38), a blessing could not be withdrawn.

Jacob's Dream

We now leave Isaac and Rebekah and Esau and begin the long trip with Jacob, "And Jacob went out from Beersheba, and went toward Haran" (28:10). Jacob had between six and seven hundred miles of rough country to cover as he moved north and slightly east from Beersheba in the southern part of present day Israel to Haran in the southern part of present day Turkey. We're not told much about this long and arduous trip except for a couple of incidents that occurred along the way.

The first came early in his journey—about fifty-five miles north of Beersheba. After making camp and settling down for the night, using a stone for a pillow, Jacob dreamed. He saw a ladder "set up on the earth, and the top of it reached to heaven" (28:12).

The Hebrew word translated "ladder" means a staircase. While we don't know for sure, it is possible he was picturing a Mesopotamian ziggurat or temple. The Mesopotamians, from whom Abraham was descended, believed that their god lived in the uppermost chamber (heaven) of the ziggurat and that the exterior staircase leading down from that high point to the ground and used by the priests was the link between earth and heaven. Though Jacob had most likely never seen a ziggurat, it is very possible that he had heard his elders describe one as they passed along stories of the land of their origin.

Next, our writer goes on to tell his readers more about what Jacob saw. We're told that "angels of God were ascending and descending on it [the ladder]." Then, as Jacob's dream continued, the Lord spoke to him and said, "I am the Lord God of Abraham thy father, and the God of Isaac." And after identifying Himself the Lord proceeded to give His blessing to Jacob. First God assures young Jacob that the land will one day be his, and He goes on to say that his descendants will be as numberless as dust and that they will be a blessing to all the world.

The dream ends with the Lord personally assuring Jacob of His presence. "I am with thee, and will keep thee in all places whither thou goest, and will bring thee again into this land; for I will not leave thee, until I have done that which I have spoken to thee of" (28:15). Notice that God did *not* say, "I will be with you as long as you go where I go." And He did *not* say, "I will be with you as long as you do what I've commanded." Rather, God promised to be with Jacob until what He had promised actually happened!

Jacob Awakens from His Dream

"And Jacob awaked out of his sleep, and he said, Surely the Lord is in this place. . . . this is none other but the house of God, and this is the gate of heaven" (28:16–17). It is obvious that Jacob was profoundly moved by his dream. Up until now God was the God of his fathers, a distant figure. Now, He is Jacob's God, He has personally revealed Himself. Undoubtedly, Jacob had heard from both his grandfather and father about *their* God, but now the Lord God was his personal God. He was filled with fear, awe, and wonder (28:17).

Marked for Life

Jacob was a long way from being what he would be someday, but he had met God and was on the way. As a reminder to himself and others, he took the stone he had used for a pillow "and set it up for a pillar, and poured oil upon the top of it" (28:18), consecrating it and making it a stele or "standing stone" to mark the place where he met God. He also gave the place a name, calling it Beth-el (beth-El), the house or dwelling place of God.

This part of the story reminds me of my Boy Scout days, when we were taught to mark our trails with small piles of stones at regular intervals. This way we could retrace our steps and avoid getting lost.

I'm reminded, too, of the many other times and places in my life when God has touched me in a particular place and by certain people. Often I didn't realize at the time the significance of those moments. But now the memory of those places and people have become "markers" in my life that keep me from getting lost.

Further proof of Jacob's deep feelings is seen in the words of his vow or promise to God (28:20–22). This solemn vow had three parts to it. First, the Lord

Excavations and ruins at Bethel. Originally named Luz, this ancient site, located about twelve miles north of Jerusalem, was where young Jacob had his dream while traveling to Padan-aram. Bethel figured prominently in the life of the Patriarchs.

would be "my God" (28:21). Second, Jacob acknowledged God's presence in that place. And, third, he promised to give the Lord a tenth of everything he had (28:22). Every part of Jacob's life was touched as a result of this meeting. At the same time, he was still the same scheming Jacob, because he made his vow on the condition that God make good on His promises. He still had to learn to trust unconditionally.

Before moving on to the next part of our lesson we must stop a moment and reflect on why God was so generous with a man like Jacob. Actually, the Scripture doesn't give us any answers. As we think back over all we know of Jacob so far, it becomes obvious that nothing he has done earned him God's blessing. But he did have a hunger for blessing.

From a human point of view Sir Francis Bacon's observation has merit, "God hangs the greatest weights upon the smallest wires." But through our spiritual eyes we see the marvelous grace of God at work. And as the Jacob story unfolds in our remaining lessons, some of the answers begin to take form.

Jacob Arrives at Haran

After leaving Bethel Jacob continued on north and slightly east to near Aleppo. From there he likely headed due east until he crossed the Euphrates where he then turned north to Haran in Padan-aram. This area was also known as Aram Naharaiim—Aram of the Two Rivers, the Euphrates and the Tigris. It was also referred to by the Hebrews as the Land of the Fathers. Our Genesis writer refers to it as "the land of the people of the east" (29:1).

You will remember that Abraham settled in Haran many years before after leaving his original home in Ur. And it was from Haran, after Terah's death, that Abraham traveled west and south down through Canaan to Shechem and on to Beersheba in the Negev.

It is thought that after Abraham left Haran that his brother Nahor followed in his footsteps and moved from Ur to the Land of the Fathers. And while that branch of Abraham's family evidently worshiped the gods of their Aramean neighbors, family ties were so close that Rebekah was chosen as Isaac's wife, and now Jacob had arrived there to find his wife.

Upon his arrival, Jacob's first stopping place was a well covered, as was the custom, by a large stone (29:2–3) to protect it from contamination, shifting sands, and unlawful "dippers." Even today many such wells are covered by slabs of stone so large and heavy that several men are needed to uncover them.

Based on the customs of that time it was perfectly natural for Jacob to stop first at the city well. The city gate and the city well were the two accepted places to meet people, and the well was preferred by the nomadic shepherds. It was there they gathered in the late afternoon to water their flocks.

In a conversation with the shepherds lounging near the well, Jacob verifies that he has arrived at Haran (29:4). When he asks if they know Laban, they volunteer some important information. It just so happens that Laban's daughter Rachel is approaching the well with some of her father's sheep (29:6).

The Shepherds at the City Well

Apparently, it only took one quick look for Jacob to see that Rachel was an exceptionally beautiful young woman. Turning back to the shepherds, he reprimanded them for not removing the stone and watering their own flocks so they'd be out of the way. But they responded that they were waiting for more shepherds to come up with their flocks so there would be more of them to remove the heavy stone (29:7–8).

Just then Rachel arrived with her father's sheep, and with that, Jacob did a little bit of grandstanding by single-handedly removing the heavy stone covering, drawing water to fill the troughs for Rachel and "the flock of Laban his mother's brother" (29:10).

Our Genesis writer doesn't give us any kind of a clue as to Rachel's reactions to this stranger's behavior, but undoubtedly she was more than a little surprised. After the sheep had all been watered, her amazement had to be compounded when the stranger kissed her and told her that he was her Aunt Rebekah's son (29:11–12).

The storyteller doesn't fill in any further details

The Meeting with Rachel

about what happened to the sheep. He merely tells us that Rachel rushed home to tell her father the good news about her cousin's arrival from far-off Canaan.

Laban Meets His Nephew Jacob

As soon as the news of Jacob's arrival reached Laban, he hurried out to the city well to welcome his nephew in lavish Near Eastern style, and escorted Jacob "to his house" (29:13). This little detail says a lot about Laban's station in Haran. Ordinary flock owners and shepherds lived in tents so they could move easily to different feeding places. But Laban is a wealthy clan chieftain so he enjoyed the luxury of a house while his hired shepherds moved from place to place with the sheep.

Excavations of Haran ruins reveal the presence of odd-shaped one-room houses made of stone. It was probably to such a house that Laban took his young nephew. There they celebrated his arrival for a full month. Such celebrations were typical of the culture, but Laban may also have been working on an angle of his own. In all probability he was well aware of the wealth Isaac had inherited from his father Abraham, and now he was entertaining Abraham's grandson and heir right there in his own home. It is very possible the gleam in his eye was related to the fact that he had *two* daughters of marriageable age.

A Tale of Two Brides

After the month of celebration, Laban got down to business. It was apparently already agreed that Jacob would work for him, but the matter of wages had to be settled (29:15). Jacob responded immediately. Rather than take pay, he would like to work out the dowry for Rachel. In a few words the storyteller sums up Jacob's proposal, "And Jacob loved Rachel; and said, I will serve thee seven years for Rachel thy younger daughter" (29:18).

Now the purpose of Jacob's trip to Haran was clear. Laban may have suspected it before, but now he knew. And his response to Jacob's request gives us an early clue to his tricky nature: "It is better that I give *her* to thee, than that I should give her to another man: abide with me" (29:19, italics mine). Notice, Jacob specified Rachel; Laban's response omitted Rachel's name.

With the sealing of this agreement Jacob became his uncle's unpaid servant. Thinking that he had cut an honest deal, Jacob settled down for seven years of hard work as a shepherd, but he was so much in love with Rachel that, the writer tells us, those years seemed as if they were only a few days. Then, as soon as he had served his time, Jacob said to his uncle, "Give me my wife, for my days are fulfilled, that I may go in unto her" (29:21).

Laban agreed, and invited all his neighbors and workers to the wedding celebration. That evening, after the festivities, he delivered a veiled bride to Jacob. Only with the morning light did Jacob discover that he had been deceived. He had married and spent the night with Leah, Laban's unattractive older daughter (29:17, 23–25). Jacob angrily confronted his uncle over this switch tactic, but is calmly told that in their culture the youngest daughter in a family cannot marry before the oldest. (This was the custom in the Mesopotamian region at that time.) In other words, what had happened was perfectly normal. Obviously, tricky Jacob had met his equal in his uncle.

After justifying his actions Laban then went on to tell Jacob that he could have Rachel by working for him another seven years. We know nothing of the details of those seven years except that Jacob worked them out and received Rachel as his wife. After fourteen years of hard work, his goal was achieved. But now he had two wives! That was not unusual for the culture of the times. We're told, however, that he loved Rachel more than Leah (29:27–30).

Jacob's Sons

At the end of fourteen years Jacob had paid off the dowry on his two wives. Now he was debt free, but he continued working with his uncle for another six or so years (31:40). And now, compacted into a few verses (29:31–30:24) we have detailed the birth of eleven sons and one daughter.

We're first told that Rachel, the much-loved wife,

47

was not able to get pregnant, but Leah had no such problem. In just a few words the Genesis writer tells of the birth of her first four sons. The firstborn she names Reuben, which means "behold a son." Her second son she calls Simeon, "God has heard." Levi, the name of the third son, may mean "attached"— Leah hoped that with his birth Jacob would feel more attached to her. When she gave birth to a fourth son, she named him Judah, which means "praise the Lord."

While mention of God has been fairly absent from this tale of love and deceit, we can see a purpose to it if we remember the writer's main purpose in telling the story. Throughout we see that God's plans are being accomplished in spite of the deceit and the manipulation by people. God's mercy on the homely and unloved Leah has produced a son named Judah, the ancestor of both David the king and Jesus the Messiah. So often God's great acts begin with the common life of one man or woman.

We come now to a major household clash. Envying her sister, and feeling sorry for herself, Rachel lashes out at Jacob (30:1), demanding that he give her the children she wants so badly. Jacob's response is as uncreative as Rachel's; he flares up in anger, telling her that her inability to have children is a judgment of God that he can't do anything about (30:2).

In her desperation Rachel resorted to a very common practice of that day in the Near East by having Jacob sleep with her slave girl, Bilhah. You will remember that years before Sarah had resorted to the same tactic with her maid Hagar. Bilhah became pregnant, and her son was born "upon Rachel's knees," making him technically her son. Rachel named him Dan, which comes from the Hebrew word that means vindication or justice. Still unable to conceive, Rachel repeats the process, and Bilhah bears a second son whom Rachel names Naphtali, meaning "fought" or "wrestled." Now Rachel felt she was winning out over her sister (30:3–8).

During this time Leah was also unable to get pregnant again, so she too gave her slave girl, Zilpah, to Jacob. Zilpah conceived and bore a son for Leah, who named him Gad, which means "good fortune" (30:9–11). Then Zilpah had a second son whom Leah named Asher—"happy" (30:12–13).

In verses 14 to 16 we have a strange bit of maneuvering between Rachel and Leah. Apparently the reference here is to a rare root that was thought to have fertility power. The outcome is another son for Leah whom she names Issachar, which means to "hire for wages" (30:16–18). Next we're told that Leah had two more children—Zebulun whose name means "gift," and a daughter, Dinah (30:20–21).

Meanwhile, Rachel has finally gotten pregnant—not because of any magic potions or fertility drugs but because "God remembered" her (30:22). This son is named Joseph which means "may God add," implying that she is yet to have another son (30:24). And, as we shall see a little later, she was right (35:16).

Possibly you have noticed the writer has carefully said at each point that the mothers named the children. This was very much in line with the custom of the ancient Near East. Also, I'm sure you have noticed that each name has a special meaning. Genealogy and names were most important to the people in those times. Since family names weren't used, the surnames given were intended to reflect the person's character and nature. We will see this illustrated again in a future lesson as Jacob himself undergoes a name change that indicates a character change.

A Guide to Our Understanding

The writer of Genesis gives us this very human story of the rivalry of two women whose children's names document their ups and downs. But there is very little religious commentary imposed on the story. What we gain from its study is the realization that the tribes of Israel that would emerge in the future were not stylized, artificial territorial units, but the extensions of real human beings.

Recently, my wife Jackie and I traveled to British Columbia, the beautiful, westernmost province of Canada. This was our first visit and we knew very little about the scenery, the people, and their life-style. During our eight-day visit we toured museums, viewed the magnificent scenery, and met a lot of friendly people. Now, British Columbia isn't just a Canadian province on our map. Rather, it has become a real place with a rich culture, beautiful country, and unique people whom we've been privileged to know just a little.

The study of biblical personalities—our spiritual ancestors—can help us get to know these characters as real people. But above all, our study can help us realize that we respond to the same God as they, in much the same ways. And this same God responds to us with the same quality of mercy and justice as He did with them in ancient times. In this way, their story becomes our story, which is all a part of God's story.

Jacob's Possessions

The focus shifts now from the story of how Jacob's family has grown and prospered during his years in Padan-aram to his material prosperity—all of which had been promised by the Lord. At least fourteen years have passed since Jacob had first started to work for his uncle. He has prospered in every way, but following Joseph's birth Jacob makes it clear to Laban that he wants to leave and return to his old home in southern Canaan (30:25).

On the surface, we would think that Jacob would just assemble his family and herds and leave, but it wasn't that simple. There were two kinds of marriages in the ancient Near East at that time. The first and most common practice was for the wife to leave her home and join her husband's family. However, in the second kind of marriage the husband left his own people and joined his wife's family clan. This was the arrangement Jacob had with Laban, and according to the custom of that time and place, everything Jacob owned, including his wives and children, were his father-in-law's property.

With this information in hand we can better understand why Jacob didn't just leave and take everything he owned with him. In addition to asking Laban's permission to go, he also pleads for the release of his wives and children (30:26). In effect Jacob was asking his father-in-law to release him from the contractural agreement they had.

It had become pretty obvious to Laban, as he had watched his nephew over the years, that Jacob had not only prospered in his own right but that he had been at least partially responsible for the business success of the whole clan. Consequently, Laban begs his son-in-law to stay with him and even goes so far as to ask Jacob to set his own wages (30:27–28).

Then begins some pretty crafty bargaining. And it ends with Jacob seemingly giving Laban the best deal. He would continue to look after all of their combined herds, but he would get to keep as his own all of the mottled or speckled sheep while Laban would keep the unblemished solid color sheep. Laban decided this was a pretty good deal because in his experience most healthy sheep were born solid colored. So the bargain is struck with each one thinking he had outdone the other (30:29–36).

Then comes some grand maneuvering. Years before Laban had had his day when he got the best of Jacob by slipping Leah into his tent instead of Rachel on that first wedding night. This had cost Jacob another seven years out of his life. Now, tricky Jacob sets up a scheme, that seems pretty ludicrous to us, to control the color of the healthy sheep (30:37–43). However, this genetic juggling occurred, the end result was that more healthy spotted sheep were born than any other kind. Jacob turned out to be the winner while Laban was the loser. Our writer drops the curtain on this episode by saying, "And the man [Jacob] increased exceedingly, and had much cattle, and maidservants, and menservants, and camels, and asses." This period of Jacob's life covered about six more years (31:41).

Jacob's Escape

The rest of our story for this lesson (Chapter 31) is devoted to describing just how Jacob finally got away from Padan-aram and from Laban's custody. The Genesis writer unravels this tale in three movements: Jacob's reason for leaving (31:1–16); the departure itself (31:17–25); and, the details of Jacob's last contract and covenant with Laban (31:26–55).

In the first movement of this story we learn that Jacob had three reasons for wanting to leave at this particular time. Two of the reasons have human origins, the third is divine. Jacob was convinced it was time to leave—and in a hurry—first because of the anger and resentment of Laban's sons. They felt Jacob had taken advantage of their father (31:1). After all, their own inheritance was being cut into by their crafty brother-in-law.

Second, it appears that Laban finally woke up to what had happened. The Genesis writer, seemingly with tongue in cheek, gives us a marvelously understated description of Laban's attitude, "And Jacob beheld the countenance of Laban, and, behold, it was not toward him as before" (31:2). Things were getting tense.

The third reason for Jacob's determination to leave was a direct command from God. The Lord told Jacob to return to his homeland and then added, "I will be with thee" (31:3). I think it is important to note that God's promise to be with Jacob didn't constitute His approval of Jacob's tactics. Rather, this is a marvelous illustration of God's grace as He works out His plan for people. How fortunate most of us are that we don't necessarily always get what we deserve. Happily, God's grace is just as active today as it was thirty-five hundred years ago.

Jacob's next move in this saga is to call a family council in which he sets out persuasively to turn Leah and Rachel against their father so they will be willing to leave. First he exaggerates Laban's tricky actions, and then he rationalizes his own success by claiming that God has approved of his actions and that is why he has been successful. That tactic has a very up-to-date sound. A common ploy is to engineer something for selfish reasons and then credit God for our success (31:4–13).

Jacob's arguments are successful. Leah and Rachel agree they, too, have lost standing with their father—he hasn't been fair with them either. So, they agree to stick with Jacob and rationalize that God is with them because of Jacob's success (31:14–16). The decision is made; they will all slip away together.

Laban's Last Cause

The stage is set when Laban is away from home to attend to shearing his flocks. Now is the hour! Jacob collects his family and everything he owns. In vivid language the storyteller writes, "Jacob stole away unawares . . . he fled with all he had . . . and passed over the river (the Euphrates), and set his face toward the mount Gilead" (31:20–21).

There's a little aside in verse 19 where we're told that "Rachel had stolen the images that were her father's." We're not told why she did this, but her actions might be tied in with the ancient Near Eastern notion that whoever had the family gods could claim the inheritance and the rights of leadership in the clan.

Three days later Laban is tipped off to what has happened. As might be expected, he gathers together some members of the family and takes off in hot pursuit to claim what he considers to be his. But before he could catch up with the slow moving caravan Laban is warned by God in a dream not to either hinder or harm Jacob (31:22–24).

The confrontation when Laban catches up with Jacob has strong overtones of humor. He calls Jacob a cheat and thief, while at the same time telling him that if they hadn't slipped away secretly, he might have sent them joyfully away with songs and music (31:25–28).

Jacob's Last Bargain with Laban

As the harangue continues, Laban first admits that God has told him not to harm Jacob, and then he lashes out at his son-in-law for stealing the household gods. In spite of Jacob's denial, Laban frantically goes through all of the baggage without success. The writer of Genesis gives us the comical scene of Laban being outwitted by his daughter. When he comes to Rachel's tent, she is calmly sitting on a stack of baggage and informs her father that she cannot be disturbed because "the custom of women is upon me"—it is her menstrual time. Laban believes her—and so she keeps him from finding the stolen idols stashed away in the luggage she is sitting on (31:29–35).

In this scene Rachel certainly reminds us of Eve her first ancestor who after taking the forbidden fruit from the Tree of Knowledge attempted to conceal her guilt from God with a lie (Gen. 3:13). In reality, the lesson for us is that we can't hide anything from God, for He is the One "from whom no secrets are hid." But before we are too quick with our condemnation of either Eve or Rachel we might ask ourselves, "What things in my life would I like to hide from God?"

It is clear to Jacob now that he has the upper hand, and he takes full advantage by unleashing a strong tirade against his frustrated father-in-law. In his litany of bitterness Jacob rehearses how Laban had taken advantage of him over the last twenty years (31:36–42). If Laban had had his way, Jacob says, he would have left Padan-aram empty handed.

Without the household gods, Laban's symbol of authority, he has no legal claim against Jacob, so he presses for a bargain—a covenant (31:43–44). He asks for Jacob's word that he will always care for Laban's daughters and grandchildren. For all of his cunning and deceptive character, Laban loved his family and wanted the assurance they would be well cared for.

The Bargain Is Sealed

Agreement is reached and the men use two ancient customs to seal their contract. They erect a stone pillar or stele and then heap up a pile of stones beside it to mark the meeting place. Then they join together in a ritual meal indicating that agreement had been reached and that neither one would cross the boundary of stones and violate the other's territory (31:45–54).

As was customary at that time, the parties to the agreement gave the place where it was ratified a special name. In Laban's Chaldean language it was Jegar-sahadutha and in Jacob's Hebrew it was Galeed. In both languages the names meant "The heap of witness."

Following the ceremony Laban adds to the bargain by saying, "The Lord watch between me and thee, when we are absent one from another" (31:49). Today these now familiar words are often used as a benediction, but it is quite likely that for Laban and

Jacob they could loosely be translated, "I can't trust you out of my sight, so remember that the Lord has His eye on you!" They are words of warning rather than of blessing.

It is also worth noting here that as a part of this agreement, Jacob was not to marry any other wives. This clause assured Laban that his daughters' children would be the sole beneficiaries of Jacob's vast wealth (31:50).

Finally, the provisions of the agreement or covenant were solemnized as Jacob pledged his word by the God of Abraham and Laban by the Semitic deities he worshiped. The pledge of both men was now sacred (31:53).

"And early in the morning Laban rose up, and kissed his sons and his daughters, and blessed them: and Laban departed, and returned unto his place" (31:55). In this last scene we have Laban's graceful acceptance of peace with Jacob, and Jacob's honest commitment to care for and protect Laban's children and grandchildren. In all of this we see that God really has the last word in what has been a sad story of treachery, deceit, and one-upmanship.

Jacob and Laban part company with mutual understanding, if not friendship. While not an ideal relationship, it is a vast improvement over what had happened between Jacob and Esau some twenty years earlier when they parted with such bitterness and hatred. Perhaps in this we catch a glimpse of God's grace at work in Jacob—a step toward the drastic change that will occur in the next lesson.

What do we learn from this thirty-five-hundred-year-old story? Of primary importance, I think, is the way God works out His purposes through very ordinary and even defective human beings (the only kind there are). This is the continuing story of Genesis—and of our own lives. God's patience and grace and blessing follow us as they did Jacob.

Lord, Thank You for Your grace, for continually working through me as if I am already the person You're helping me to become. AMEN.

WHAT THIS SCRIPTURE MEANS TO ME
Genesis 27:46—31:55

July 7, 1982, was not a good day for me. My husband and I had lived in Waco, Texas, for only one week. My Michigan blood hadn't adjusted to the hot and humid weather, and many of our belongings were still in boxes scattered around the house, so I was feeling very unsettled.

Earlier that day I had gone to a nearby mall to buy wastebaskets and other necessities for the house and to get my hair cut. While waiting for my hair appointment, I passed the time on one of the mall benches and worked on a needlepoint kneeler for the chapel of the seminary my husband attended.

When it was time for me at the beauty salon, I carelessly left the bag containing this needlework project on the bench. Only a few moments had passed when I realized this, but when I returned to the bench, there was no sign of this valuable piece of work.

Later that afternoon when I got home a call came from my parents telling me that my brother had seriously injured his foot while mowing the lawn.

By this time, my emotions were completely strung out. I felt bombarded by events that seemed totally out of my control. Everything was going wrong. I wanted to escape.

Since I didn't yet know my way around Waco, I decided to go to Skaggs Alpha Beta, a grocery store two blocks from our house. With no checking account and only $13.47 to my name, I made a mental list of the items I would buy. As I made my selections, I tried to keep track of how much I was spending. But several minutes later, the ultimate nightmare occurred. I had overspent my $13.47. The cashier waited impatiently while I counted out the change. Very embarrassed and at the point of tears, I told her to deduct the seventy-five cent birthday card I had bought.

Without saying a word, the elderly man behind me reached into his pocket. As he handed me a crumpled dollar bill, he said, "Here, I want you to send that birthday card."

Four years have gone by since that poorly dressed but kind gentleman handed me that dollar, but I've never forgotten it. It wasn't the money but his desire to help someone in distress. Without expecting anything in return, he freely gave a part of what he had.

It is this "spirit of giving" that impressed me as I read Jacob's words, "and of all that thou shalt give me I will surely give the tenth unto thee" (Gen. 28:22). Jacob had just experienced God's presence in a dream and had heard His promise, "Behold, I am with thee, and will keep thee in all places whither thou goest" (Gen. 28:15). His sense of awe, reverence, and gratitude led him to make this sincere pledge to God.

Several years ago, Jacob's words about tithing inspired me to seriously evaluate my own attitude toward giving. As a result, my financial pledge to the church increased considerably. That is a decision I have never regretted.

Next, I decided to try to give more of myself to the church and to the community. This has given me some wonderfully rich experiences as I've cooked and delivered food for Meals on Wheels, made phone calls to elderly people in our congregation, and have become involved in several local relief agencies.

Through all of these experiences I've learned that we can't outgive God. Out of His abundance He gives us life, and as we return a portion to Him by helping others, He gives us a richer and fuller life than we could ever have imagined possible. "Thank you, Lord."

LESSON 3
GENESIS 32:1–36:43

Jacob's Search for Peace

Father God, Help me to have my peace in You, and help me to deliberately seek peace with my brother. AMEN.

Our lesson opens now with Jacob and his slow moving caravan heading south and slightly west toward his final destination in southern Canaan. It is most likely that uppermost in his own mind is the dread of the inevitable meeting with his brother.

But first, the Genesis writer tells us that Jacob's caravan is met by a host or army of angels (32:1–2). Our Scripture lesson doesn't give us any clue as to why the angels intercepted Jacob at this point or whether any message or word of warning was issued. We do know that on two or three earlier occasions angels had been involved in Jacob's life. Probably the most awesome experience had been at Bethel more than twenty years before when in his dream, Jacob saw angels ascending and descending the ladder. Later an angel had told him to leave Padan-aram (31:11).

It doesn't take much imagination to assume that this dramatic meeting profoundly affected Jacob's thinking. He refers to meeting God's host or as other translations word it, "God's camp" or "God's company." We are told that Jacob gave the meeting place a name—"Mahanaim," which means two camps or two companies. It is likely Mahanaim was located just east of the Jordan River and north of the Jabbok River on the caravan route east of Succoth.

We don't know what else happened at Mahanaim, except that Jacob immediately dispatched messengers to travel south to Edom with a message for Esau (32:3). The message was straight to the point: Jacob had acquired great wealth and position during his years in Padan-aram which included large herds of cattle and flocks of sheep as well as many servants (32:4–5). Jacob wanted Esau to know that he was headed for his old home in the Negev, on the west side of Jordan and wanted to be at peace with his brother.

Esau's Coming

When Jacob's messengers returned from their mission, their report wasn't what he had hoped for. Not only had they found Esau but even now he was on the way to meet Jacob, and he had an army of four hundred men with him (32:6). The Genesis writer tells us that "Jacob was greatly afraid and distressed" (32:7). Other translators have described him as being frantic with fear. Today we'd probably say he was scared to death.

I once asked a group of small children what they would do if the Lord came to visit their house. Several gave the expected response, "I'd say hello and let Him in," "I'd give Him a cookie." But a small, curly-headed little girl looked up and said, "I'd be scared silly." I think her answer best describes Jacob, and us, when we face the unknown or expect the worst.

Jacob's Plan to Save Himself

His many years of conniving and manipulation now helped Jacob surface with a plan he hoped would work (32:7–8). He would divide up his caravan—people and herds—into groups or companies and send them out ahead. His reasoning was clear, "If Esau come to the one company, and smite it, then the other company which is left shall escape."

Having done that, Jacob decided it was time to

pray to the God of his fathers for help (32:9–12). In his prayer Jacob reminds the Lord that He had instructed him to return to south Canaan. He admitted that he didn't deserve the Lord's mercy, but, after all, years before he had been assured that his descendants would be so numerous they couldn't be counted. And specifically he pressed his point home, "Deliver me, I pray thee, from the hand of my brother, from the hand of Esau: *for I fear him,* lest he will come and smite me, and the mother with the children" (32:11, italics mine).

There can be no doubt about the fervency of Jacob's prayer. We don't know just how much praying Jacob had been doing over the last twenty years, but things looked pretty desperate now, so he really prayed. I suspect there's a lot of Jacob in most of us. We tend to become careless until we're up against it, and then our thoughts turn to God. I sometimes wonder how different we would be if our prayers of thanksgiving were as urgent as our prayers for help?

The next morning after he had put together his plan and prayed, Jacob selected some of his choice flocks and sent them in several droves with his servants ahead of the rest of the company. As each drove was intercepted by Esau, the servants were to tell him that they were a gift from Jacob (31:13–18), and that Jacob himself with his wives and children were following behind (21:19–20). It was Jacob's hope, of course, that such a lavish series of gifts would soften his brother up and prevent the slaughter of the clan.

After the advance group had left, Jacob then instructed the other companies to go on ahead, spaced out so they wouldn't be all together. Each was told to identify themselves to Esau and tell him that Jacob was coming up in the rear with his wives and children (32:19–20). The stage was now set for the dramatic meeting. It was Jacob's hope that as each contingent with the offer of gifts met his brother, peace would be possible.

Again, we see ourselves in so much of this story. How often we have attempted to buy the good graces of someone we've slighted or injured with a gift-payoff of one kind or another! It is terribly easy for us to be judgmental of Jacob or someone we know unless we take the time to examine our own motives.

Finally, in the cool of the evening Jacob took his wives and children and forded the Jabbok (32:22–23). Then he evidently sent them on ahead a little ways to camp while he stayed behind. And at this point the writer injects a strong note of pathos into the story when he says, "Jacob was left alone." There's something about this scene that reminds me of the picture of George Washington alone on his knees praying in the snow at Valley Forge.

So often in the dark nights of my soul, that picture of Washington has flashed across the screen of my mind. Yes, I'm aware of the snow and of the expression on the general's face. But what stands out most vividly is the aloneness of the man on his knees.

History tells us the story of a beleaguered Washington who had suffered one defeat after another, moving his troops into winter quarters at Valley Forge. The situation was desperate. The Continental Army was suffering from atrocious food, bitter cold, inadequate clothing and supplies, and the carping criticism of members of Congress hovered over Washington like a dark cloud.

From the artist's viewpoint General Washington was very much alone. But not really. The events of history indicate God was with him.

The writer of Genesis doesn't tell us here why Jacob stayed behind, alone. Perhaps the past was catching up with him and he knew he had to come to terms with it by himself. But he turned out not to be alone, because he spent the whole night wrestling with a "man . . . until the breaking of the day" (32:24). At this point we are given no clues as to who the "man" is. But something about the darkness of night makes any kind of wrestling encounter more scary, especially one with an unknown opponent. In spite of all the odds against him (Jacob was at least sixty years old—see 26:34), Jacob hung on to his assailant, refusing to give in but unable to gain an upper hand.

Finally, as it was beginning to get light, the "man"

Jacob's Long Night

touched Jacob's thigh and crippled him. Yet still Jacob held on, probably suspecting now that the One he was grasping so tightly was more than a mere man.

"Let me go," said his opponent.

"I will not let thee go, except thou bless me," Jacob replied.

Here is Jacob, the heel-grabber or snatcher, still holding on for dear life, still demanding the blessing. But these seemingly negative characteristics turn out to be strengths as well as weaknesses. But before he can *receive* the blessing one more thing is required of Jacob.

"What is thy name?" the wrestler asked him.

The last time Jacob was asked that question, he lied. He was unable to admit to being who he was. Now however, he replies, "Jacob" (32:27).

When a Hebrew in those days gave someone his name, it was an act of submission. In other words, the "man" is really saying to Jacob, "Give me control over your life."

Once when I was getting ready to shop for a car,

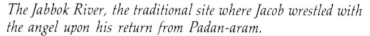

The Jabbok River, the traditional site where Jacob wrestled with the angel upon his return from Padan-aram.

A view of the Jabbok River, present-day Wadi Zerqa. The Jabbok flows west and enters the Jordan River about twenty-five miles north of the Dead Sea. It was just south of the Jabbok where Jacob and Esau had their dramatic meeting.

a friend told me, "Don't give salesmen your name and address right away, unless you want to be called at home." In other words, when we tell who we really are, we are inviting others into our lives and in a sense are surrendering a certain amount of control.

This time Jacob exposed his identity. But instead of condemnation came these surprising words: "Thy name shall be called no more Jacob, but Israel" (32:28). Jacob, the supplanter, is now Israel, a prince of God, or (probably a better translation), the one who persevered with God, the one who struggled with God. And not only a struggler, but someone with power, who prevails.

In the ancient Near East a person's name indicated something about his character. In this scene, even though details are sparse, the change of Jacob's name symbolizes a conversion experience. As God took possession of Jacob that night, he became a new person; he had a new identity.

Suddenly Jacob's unknown opponent is on his side—yet still unknown. As is natural, Jacob wants to know his blesser's name. The reply is, in effect, "You shouldn't ask." And then Jacob knew, for he named the site of this encounter Peniel—the place where he saw God face to face and still lived— (32:30). As "the sun rose upon him," a beautiful symbol of new life, Jacob limped away from his contest with God. Being crippled became a constant reminder to him that he could never step ahead of God, and win.

The Dramatic Meeting

We come now in our lesson to one of the most dramatic and emotional scenes in the Bible. For over twenty years Jacob had dreaded the prospect of meeting his brother again. Now that meeting was about to take place. Jacob had assumed his brother was on the war path. And we can be sure that he kept his eyes glued to the horizon—ever watchful for the approach of his brother and the four hundred men that were reported to be with him.

Movement in the distance warned Jacob that the moment of confrontation was close at hand, so he divided up his family into three groups. The first group was made up of the maidservants, Bilhah and Zilpah, and their children. They were put in the frontline out from the camp. Next, at timed intervals came Leah and her children, and then Rachel and Joseph (33:2–3). What a sight this must have been— bleating sheep, fearful and crying children, and sullen adults, all forced to stand in line under the hot sun as they waited to face an unknown fate.

Now, however, we see a new Jacob. Instead of hiding behind his wives and children, as he had planned at first, he strode past them and ahead of the first group to meet his brother face to face. They met, Jacob bowed low to Esau seven times. It was the custom of that time for Canaanite chieftains to pay respect to their superiors by bowing seven times. Aramean custom provided for one very low bow.

Jacob's massive show of humility was certainly meant to impress his brother and take the edge off his anger.

But Jacob wasn't the only one who had changed—Esau had changed too. We read that Esau ran to meet him, and embraced him, and "fell on his neck"—hugged him—"and kissed him: and they wept" (33:4). The evil of the past was forgotten in that moment; they were brothers again. I wonder if Jesus had this story in the back of his mind when he told the parable of the prodigal son, and described the father running to meet his lost son.

Israel—A New Man

As the rest of the family witnessed this unexpected sight, no doubt moving closer for a better look, Esau looked up and saw the crowd of women, children, and animals that made up this part of Jacob's caravan. "Who are those?" he asks. These are "the children which God hath graciously given thy servant" (33:5), responds Jacob.

Imagine Esau's amazement. He knew that Jacob had left home a little over twenty years before with nothing. At that time Esau had vowed to kill him on sight. Now, it was obvious that Jacob had prospered—God had indeed blessed him in spite of himself. And now the meeting between the two brothers was peaceful. What a change!

In his one sentence response to Esau Jacob clearly gives God credit for all he has and refers to himself as a servant. Indeed a miracle had occurred—cunning and arrogant Jacob now calls himself "thy servant." God had truly met Jacob at Peniel. In this changed Jacob, now Israel, we have a servanthood-model for our lives.

Grace Will Lead Me Home

Next we read that each of the three companies of family moved forward and presented themselves to Esau (33:6–7). And as Esau meets them, he asks Jacob to explain the purpose of this entourage. Jacob doesn't admit that he had lined his family up this way out of fear, and in response to why Jacob had sent ahead the large herd of animals—"All this drove which I met"—Jacob explains, "These are to find

A view of the mountains of Edom (Sier). It was in this rugged country that Esau went to live, to the south of the Dead Sea. It was from Edom that Esau came for his meeting with Jacob.

grace in the sight of my lord" (33:8)—they had been sent as a gift to soften up Esau.

Now, though, we have further evidence of the change in Esau, for he responds immediately that he has enough—he, too, has prospered (33:9). In anticipation of this meeting Jacob had expected the worst from his brother because he didn't expect the best from God. He had spent twenty years expecting his brother's revenge, but what really happened was an act of grace, and it took Jacob entirely by surprise. Grace can never be engineered, only enjoyed.

What judgment and punishment couldn't change in all of Jacob's years, love and grace accomplished in a few moments of time. Now Jacob is so overcome with relief that he begs Esau to accept his gifts. "I have seen thy face, as though I had seen the face of God." And Esau, knowing that Jacob's offer is from the heart, graciously accepts it (33:10–11).

I remember so well what it was like to see my son's face for the first time in the hospital delivery room. After nine months of waiting and wondering, it was like seeing all of the joy of the Lord wrapped up in one little bundle. Every once in a while God had favored Jacob with a glimpse of His glory—at Bethel when he saw the stairway to heaven, at the first sight of Rachel at the well, at Peniel when he wrestled with the "man," and now in the face of an enemy who had become a friend. In all of this, Jacob had learned to see God in a new way—and what a difference it made!

Jacob Goes in Peace

The next movement in our story pictures the brothers separating from each other in peace. Esau offers to escort Jacob's slower moving and unprotected caravan, but Jacob refuses his brother's generous offer. Then Esau offers to leave some of his men with Jacob for protection, but again, Jacob refuses (33:13–15). For Jacob it is enough to be at peace with his brother. And with that Esau heads south to his home in Seir.

Jacob, in turn, moves west a short distance and settles for a time in Succoth where the herds could graze in lush pastures for a few months or years before they started on the last leg of their journey that would take them across the Jordan River and into Canaan. It is hard for us with all of our fast travel and instant results to picture Jacob's slow-moving caravan. But Jacob had waited this long to realize God's promise, so he viewed time and distance quite differently from the way we do.

Moving rapidly now the Genesis writer tells us that in due time Jacob and his family forded the Jordan River and settled for a time in Shechem even as his grandfather Abraham had done many years before when he arrived in Canaan from Haran. This was an ideal location for a wealthy chieftain who had large herds of cattle and flocks of sheep to care for. Shechem was located in a valley rich with good pastureland fed by streams that had their source in nearby Mount Gerizim and Mount Ebal.

It would appear that Jacob had hopes of settling down here, at least for a time, because we are also told that he bought and paid for "a parcel of a field" so he'd have a place to live and to feed his flocks (33:18–19). Also, as his grandfather had done before him, Jacob immediately erected an altar to God who was really now his God—the God of Israel.

After the turbulence of his experiences in Padanaram and the trauma of his meeting with his brother, it would appear now that Jacob could be comfortable with himself and his surroundings. He was safely back in the country promised first to his grandfather, then to his father, and finally to him. But as we will see in the next part of our lesson, the peace and calm were not to last.

The Rape of Dinah

We come now to a sordid chapter in our story—the rape of Dinah, Jacob's only daughter by Leah and what happened because of it. All of Genesis 34 is given to this event. We'll treat this incident briefly and then move on to Isaac's last days, which sets the stage for the Joseph story that occupies the rest of Genesis.

In just a few words we are told that a young Canaanite named Shechem, a local prince, was attracted to young Dinah, "He took her, and lay with her, and defiled her" (34:2). In other words, Shechem raped this young Hebrew girl. But we're also told that he loved her and wanted to marry her (34:3–4).

Then as the story unfolds, Hamor, Shechem's father, comes to Jacob and proposes not only that he let Dinah marry his son but that they form an alliance whereby they would be at peace with each other and their children would intermarry. Shechem even tells Jacob to set a dowry figure, and whatever it is he will pay it (34:5–12).

Although such an alliance between Canaanites and Hebrews might make political sense, for followers of God to be joined with pagans would have gone against everything the Patriarchs believed. So now Jacob is put to the test. Will he compromise or hold steady to what is right?

This kind of test has been put to God's people from the beginning of time, and it is still one that we all face in the twentieth century. For the Christian to

Above are two views of the ancient site of Shechem, Jacob's first stop in Canaan after crossing the Jordan. Shechem is located in a valley in central Palestine between Mount Ebal and Mount Gerizim, about thirty-two miles north of Jerusalem.

compromise God's highest will and purpose is an invitation to disaster, even though it may come in different forms.

A Family Gets Revenge

When Jacob first heard that his daughter had been raped by Shechem, the Canaanite, his sons were not at home, so he didn't commit himself one way or another. But when they "came out of the field," that is, came home from shepherding the flocks, they were indignant (34:7). They wouldn't let their sister become involved with an uncircumcised pagan, and they wouldn't accept the idea of intermarriage. Publicly, though, they appeared to go along with Hamor's offer, providing all of the men in the city would submit to being circumcised (34:15–17). The Canaanites accepted the conditions, thinking of all the benefits they would receive from intermarrying with such a wealthy clan. All the males were circumcised, and by so doing walked right into the trap Jacob's sons had set. While the men were still recovering from the circumcision, "Simeon and Levi, Dinah's brethren, took each man his sword, and came upon the city boldly, and slew all the males. And they slew Hamor and Shechem his son with the edge of the sword, and took Dinah out of Shechem's house." In addition, they plundered the wealth of the city, "and all their little ones, and their wives took they captive" (34:25–29).

This grisly tale of rape and revenge underscores the message of Genesis—humankind has fallen far from the peaceable place that God intended. Even Jacob is shocked at the violence of his son's actions (34:30). And he is fearful that the other Canaanites will get the idea of revenge and spring a retaliatory attack on him.

Prepare the Way of the Lord

We come now in this latter part of our lesson (Chapter 35) to a brief overview of those last years of Jacob's life. It opens as once more Jacob has a direct word from the Lord, "And God said unto Jacob, Arise, go up to Bethel, and dwell there: and make there an altar unto God, that appeared unto thee when thou fleddest from the face of Esau thy brother" (35:1). Now Jacob knows that he cannot settle down in Shechem but is to break camp and make his way to Bethel where God had appeared to him the first time.

We know from our biblical history that Bethel became a very special place in Israel in later years. The Hebrews made religious pilgrimages to Bethel, but first they would purify themselves of all worldly and pagan influences. This involved changing

A picture of the site of Jacob's well as it is seen today. This was located either in Shechem or nearby and was probably dug by Jacob. In New Testament times Jacob's well was identified as being at or near Sychar. It was here that Jesus sat and talked with the Samaritan woman (John 4:5–26).

clothes, washing, and the destruction of any foreign gods (Exod. 19:10; Josh. 24:14–18, 23).

I recall as a child how my mother always insisted that I wipe my feet on the doormat before coming into the house. We were taught as children to "clean up" before going into the house. And as more mature Christians we become aware of what needs to be "cleaned up" before entering God's house and His service.

So now, in preparation for this move on to Bethel Jacob instructs his family to put away any strange and foreign gods they may have collected since their arrival at Shechem. Apparently, some of Jacob's sons had held on to some of the plunder they had taken in Shechem. They were to get rid of any idols, "and be clean, and change your garments" (35:2). There is an ancient prayer that opens with these words, "Create in us clean hearts, O God." That's what Jacob wanted of his family.

Jacob's sons obeyed their father's command and turned over to him all of the pagan statues and jewelry they had taken from Shechem, and Jacob buried all of it under an oak tree (35:4). I wonder if Rachel ever turned in the household gods she had stolen from her father. We aren't told, but we're given a clue because of the tragedy that struck as soon as the family arrived in Bethel.

The trip from Shechem south to Bethel is covered in just a few words. While they were traveling, "the terror of God was upon the cities round about them" (35:5). We have no clue as to what the writer is referring to, but we do know that in some way God was protecting Jacob's caravan from hostile people along the way. Again God demonstrated to Jacob that he did not need to be afraid, if he trusted God.

God Appears in Jacob's Time of Loss

After an absence of many years, Jacob returns to Bethel. Here he builds an altar to God, the God of Beth-el, the personal God who had kept the promises made so many years before (35:6–7). But the joy of his arrival "home" is soon marred by two crises. First, Deborah, Rebekah's nurse, died. We have no idea where or when she joined Jacob's family. We do know that she traveled from Haran with Rebekah when she came to marry Isaac. Undoubtedly she helped care for Jacob and Esau when they were babies. Possibly she came back to Haran after Rebekah died, though Rebekah's death has not been mentioned. At any rate, Deborah had to be an old, old lady, and her death must have grieved Jacob deeply. He buried her under an oak tree which came to be called the oak of weeping (the meaning of *Allon-bachuth,* 35:8).

Once more the writer tells us that God appeared to Jacob (35:9). And once more Jacob is assured that he will be the father of a great nation and his descendants will inherit the land (35:10–12). Once more, too, God assures Jacob that in reality his name is changed, "Thy name shall not be called anymore Jacob, but Israel shall be thy name."

Following this great affirmation of God's earlier promise, Jacob erected another monument of stones to mark the place where God had appeared to him.

The second crisis that strikes Jacob is devastating. Jacob and his clan had now moved on toward a place called Ephrath, and it is here that Rachel gives birth to a second son (35:16–17). She had a difficult time, and it soon became obvious that she was going to die. Before dying, however, she, according to the custom of that time, gave her son a name—Benoni, which meant "son of my sorrow." But we're also told that Jacob renamed the child Benjamin which means "the son of my right hand" (35:18). Then we're told that she died and was buried "in the way to Ephrath, which is Bethlehem" (35:19)—the birthplace of Jesus many centuries later.

We don't know why Jacob insisted on changing the name of his new son. Some writers have suggested that he wanted to avoid any bad luck that might be associated with the name. Perhaps he did not want to be continually reminded of Rachel's death whenever he called or spoke of his son. But I think Jacob's pride was really broken once again; he had to put his trust only in the hope that God would bring his children to the honored place He had pro-

A Child Is Born in Jacob's Sorrow

73

mised them. It is possible that Jacob could see a ray of sunshine in this lastborn child, even in the darkness of his beloved Rachel's death. In later chapters we will see that next to Joseph—also Rachel's son—Benjamin was the most favored of Jacob's sons.

Jacob Buries Rachel and Isaac

Jacob buried Rachel in Bethlehem where, the writer says, her grave was marked up to his day (35:19–20). Then he continued his travels south, stopping for awhile near Edah (35:21), otherwise unknown. There Reuben, Jacob's firstborn, slept with his father's concubine Bilhah, the mother of his half-brothers Dan and Naphtali (30:6–7). The writer doesn't comment on this terrible act except to say that Jacob knew what Reuben had done. Later, on his deathbed, Jacob refused to bless Reuben, because of this sinful act (49:4).

At this point, the writer lists Jacob's sons once again, as a parallel to the list of Esau's sons which follows in chapter 36, and as a hint that we are coming to the end of one generation and passing on to another. But before we do that, we are told that Jacob, now Israel, suffers another great loss—the death of his father Isaac. Isaac was still alive when Jacob came to his father's home in Hebron (35:27). But Jacob arrived only in time to witness his father's death. Isaac lived to the ripe old age of 180, and, like his father Abraham, died "full of days," meaning that he had lived a full and abundant life. And like Abraham, who was buried by his two estranged sons Isaac and Ishmael, he is buried by his sons Esau and Jacob, who now come together at the funeral in peace (35:29).

The Legacy of Esau and Jacob

The writer of Genesis takes considerable space to honor Esau and to list his descendants (Chapter 36). While the list of names may not be too interesting to us, a quick scan will show us that Esau's family was very wealthy and produced their own royal family of grand dukes and princes.

With this family tree, we come to the end of Lesson 3 of our study of Abraham's family. The saga of Jacob's encounters with God and his estranged brother Esau has made exciting reading. What I carry away from the epic struggle is not the belief that Jacob deserved the birthright and Esau did not. Neither of Isaac's boys were candidates for sainthood. But God does not choose men who make good; He choses men *to* make good.

Jacob was often insensitive, deceitful, and self-centered, but he genuinely loved Rachel, and at least some of his children. Also, Jacob, as a rule, turned to God when he was in trouble. But in that dark night at Peniel, he placed God's blessing first in his life, even to the point of the classic struggle that occurred there which ended with God in control of his life.

Esau, on the other hand, didn't care much for his birthright, and traded it away for a moment's pleasure. Then he vowed to kill his own brother to get it back. But as the years passed, Esau's shallowness and bitterness went away, and he was able to forgive his brother and accept him with warmth and grace. Many who read this story come away from it feeling that Esau was a nicer man than Jacob, and perhaps deserved more than he got. But we learn in our Genesis studies that it is God who creates, and God who decides.

I Once Was Lost

Some time ago I saw a movie about a Vietnam veteran who lived in terrible guilt over the child he had fathered and left in Vietnam. Finally he decided to go back to Communist Vietnam to find that child.

After many delays he arrived in Vietnam only to discover thousands of lost and abandoned children, who clung to him, as if he were the father of them all. One of them, a street-wise orphan boy, helped him discover that his own child had died. The boy acted tough and uncaring because no one had ever loved him, until this ex-G.I. Joe came, seeking a lost son. Both the boy and the soldier learned in the end that love is not given by birth, but by Grace.

That veteran reminds me of Jacob, who spent his life wandering the ancient Near Eastern world, trying to escape his past and trying to secure the legacy of Abraham. In the end, he discovered that Abraham's legacy was not in finding a real fortune but in finding a real faith, not given by birth but by Grace.

The Vietnam veteran saw in a lost child the face of God; Jacob saw in a lost brother the face of God. With his discovery both could finally face their past and move into their future.

As we leave Jacob and move on to the Joseph story, let us pray—*not* that we can find God when we are lost, but that He can find us.

Lord, Let me not get so entangled with the affairs of my life that I cannot hear Your loving call to clarity and direction. AMEN.

WHAT THIS SCRIPTURE MEANS TO ME
Genesis 32:1—36:43

In July of 1986, my husband and I spent three very full days at the World's Fair in Vancouver, British Columbia. It was exceptionally crowded, but we still enjoyed the beautiful climate and scenery, and were fascinated by the interesting and educational exhibits.

One evening, as we were waiting in line to enter one of the most popular pavilions, I spotted a young Chinese boy, about four years old, who was obviously in a state of panic. He was waving his arms, grasping at air, and his little face was pale and contorted. His eyes darted from person to person in the crowd as he moaned, "Oh, oh, oh."

Thinking of my own son whom we had left at home, I stepped out of line and knelt down beside this frightened child. In a soft, shaking voice, he muttered, "Mama, Mama." I tried to comfort him by saying, "Stay here; she'll come back."

Gradually I lifted him up, hoping that he would spot his mother. I kept reassuring him, "She'll come back, sweetheart, but we need to stay right here so she can find us." He began to cry and hugged my neck.

As I talked to him, and gazed at the people around me, I noticed an usher carrying a megaphone. Still holding this terrified child, I inched toward the usher, thinking he might announce that there was a lost boy in the area. Suddenly the boy's legs tightened around my waist. "Don't move, don't move," he screamed.

Then I realized why he was so insistent that we not move. After all, just moments before I had told him we should "stay right here" so his mother would find us. He had taken me at my word, and in spite of his fear had trusted me, a stranger, because he sensed I cared for him.

This incident came to mind as I read the first twelve verses of Chapter 32. We read here that Jacob was traveling to Seir to meet his brother, Esau. He had sent messengers ahead with presents because he was afraid that Esau would attack him.

In his fear, Jacob cried out to God and begged for deliverance, for God had previously promised to bless and protect him and his descendants (Gen. 28:13–15; 32:12).

Up to this time Jacob hadn't had much personal experience with God. Actually, he was asking for God's help because of the promise God had made him many years before after his dream at Bethel (Gen. 28:12–17). But in spite of his lack of experience with God, Jacob trusted Him, believed His words, and had faith in His promise.

It was humbling and moving experience for me to have received so much trust from that little boy in Vancouver. He modeled for me the kind of trust I want to have in God as my Guide and Protector. As with Jacob in his moment of need, I need to trust in God's promises to be with me under all kinds of circumstances.

The words of this children's song are simple, but they express a profound truth:

I'm not alone, for My Father is with me;
  with me wherever I go:
Speaking words of faith, of courage and
  of love;
He's with me, He loves me, wherever I go.

Source unknown

LESSON 4
GENESIS 37:1–39:23

Joseph's Early Years

Savior, Thank You for choosing me to take on Your yoke and to learn of You. AMEN.

My son Brian is two, and he loves to watch Mr. Rogers on television. This puzzled me for a long time because Mr. Rogers isn't as exciting as some of the action cartoons, and rarely is he funny like Bugs Bunny or Ernie and Bert. But watching with Brian I've learned that Mr. Rogers does something no one else does in quite the same way. He makes each child who watches him feel that he or she is important and in fact the one person for whom the show is put on. Each one is special and is Mr. Rogers' neighbor and friend.

As we come to the story of Jacob's favorite son, Joseph, I'm reminded of how often in the Book of Genesis we are told about people who are unexpectedly chosen and considered special by God. Abraham was chosen and became God's friend. Isaac was chosen in the next generation, then Jacob. Now the same thing happens with Jacob's son by Rachel, Joseph.

The setting for the beginning of our story is the

Jacob's Favorite Son

Valley of Hebron, south of Bethel and west of the Dead Sea. Jacob has settled here, and his older sons care for his flocks of animals. By this time Joseph is seventeen years old, and, says our Genesis writer, he was loved by his father more than any other of his children (37:3). And as a symbol of that special love, Jacob "made him a coat of many colors." A better translation would be "a coat with long sleeves." Most likely it was an embroidered, full-length robe with flowing sleeves that reached to his wrists—hardly a fit work garment.

The opening scene in our present saga has young Joseph out in the field feeding the sheep with two of his half brothers who were the sons of Bilhah and Zilpah, the maidservants of Leah and Rachel. It is likely the long and monotonous days following the sheep provided ample time for the shepherds to exchange gossip—"their evil report." That's what apparently happened in this scene, and we read that young Joseph carried the gossip he heard from his brothers straight to his father.

Obviously, no talebearer or tattletale is ever very popular. And this act, along with Jacob's obvious favoritism, brought to Joseph the wrath and hatred of his brothers. The Wisdom writer warned against this kind of thing when he wrote, "The words of a talebearer are as wounds, and they go down into the innermost parts of the belly" (Prov. 18:8).

In a few words, the Genesis writer pictures Joseph as a self-centered and pampered boy who was spoiled by his aged father. At the same time he heightens the drama by picturing ten brothers who felt nothing but seething hatred for the young upstart. So we have a house divided against itself with bitter resentments running deep.

Joseph's Brothers, Jacob's Heirs

To compound the brothers' bitterness against Joseph, his favored position with Jacob brought in the question of birthright. Who would be the family heir that would eventually be the clan leader? Reuben, Jacob's first-born son, was the natural heir to Jacob's estate, just as his uncle Esau had been to Isaac's. But Reuben had sinned with one of his father's concubines (35:22) and would later be disinherited (49:3–4).

Next in line were Simeon and Levi, but they had incurred their father's great displeasure with their ruthless slaughter of the people of Shechem, after their sister Dinah had been raped (34:25–30; 49:5–7). Judah was the fourth son in line, and seemed to be Joseph's main competition for Jacob's blessing. Judah had two younger brothers, Issachar and Zebulun, and Joseph had one younger brother, Benjamin, who had lesser claims than either Judah or Joseph. Dan and Naphtali were sons of the maid Bilhah, and, like Gad and Asher, the sons of the other maid, Zilpah, had little claim to the birthright.

So the brothers could see that this young dandy might well end up with Jacob's blessing instead of one of them. For as we know, Jacob was the product of favoritism; he was his mother's favorite. And he also practiced it; he favored Rachel over Leah, and now he was favoring Rachel's children as well. Perhaps Jacob didn't see how playing favorites would produce the same results for his children as it had in his own generation. But he was wrong! For a start Joseph's brothers couldn't speak a kind word to him (37:4).

Joseph Dreams Of Glory

But the brothers' hatred really boils over when Joseph brags about a dream he has had (37:5). First of all, Joseph insists that they hear his interpretation of the dream, saying in effect, "Listen up, you guys!" (37:6). He tells them that in the dream they were all binding up sheaves at harvest time in the field, but all of their sheaves of wheat bowed down before his (37:7). The dream confirms the brothers' worst suspicions about Joseph's ambition, and they taunt him, "Shalt thou indeed reign over us?" It is almost as if they unconsciously detected a hint of what was to happen many years later when they traveled to Egypt to buy grain from their unrecognized brother (37:8).

As if that isn't enough, Joseph has a second dream even more sensational than the first. This time the sun, the moon, and eleven stars all bow down before him (37:9). With insensitive disregard for their feelings, Joseph tells his father and his brothers about this dream (37:10). Now, Jacob is offended, and protests because it is clear that everyone in the family is going to bow down before Joseph. Jacob protests the idea, and rebukes Joseph for his delusions of grandeur. But then the Genesis writer adds, "And his brothers envied him; but his father observed [remembered] the saying" (37:11). Something about the dream caused Jacob to pause and reflect.

The Plot Against Joseph

Jacob's rebuke was a mild one, but it is pretty obvious that the feeling of Joseph's brothers ran very deep. Undoubtedly, they were greatly relieved when the time came for them to move their father's flocks north to the lush pastureland near Shechem and they could get away from their spoiled and cocky brother (37:12). But as we shall soon see, the cooling off respite didn't last very long.

After the brothers had been away from Hebron for a time, Jacob, evidently concerned about their welfare, decided to send Joseph to see how they and the flocks were doing (37:13–14). But when Joseph got to Shechem, he couldn't find his brothers and a local citizen found him "wandering in the field" near where his brothers should have been. From him, Joseph learned that his brothers and the animals had moved on some twenty miles further north to Dothan (37:14–17).

Even today this area is rich in grassland and fruit orchards and is amply watered by a stream. Here a twentieth-century visitor will find a small village built on top of the debris of many centuries. Looking out from the village over the surrounding plain, it is easy to picture the tents of Jacob's sons clustered there surrounded by large flocks of sheep and goats.

As Joseph approached Dothan, his brothers spotted him in the distance. He must have been easy to recognize because of his long, embroidered robe. As they watched him coming, their hatred surged to the surface again, but this time they plotted violence as "they conspired against him to slay him" (37:18).

Their plotting took several forms. First, they decided they would kill him, throw his body into a pit, and tell their father the boy had been eaten by a wild beast—"and we shall see what will become of his dreams." These last words show that they were uneasy, and therefore derisive about Joseph's dreams. In those days people took dreams a lot more seriously than we do today. Dreams were seen as prophecies of what was to come.

Reuben Intervenes

The first plan was rejected when Reuben, the oldest brother, objected to killing Joseph (37:21). Instead, he suggested, they should just throw him into one of the water tanks hewn out of solid rock and let the boy die of thirst and starvation. That way they would get rid of him without actually murdering him themselves. Then we are let in on what was actually on Reuben's mind—he would slip back later after the other brothers were gone in order to rescue Joseph and "deliver him to his father again" (37:22).

We might well ask why would Reuben want to spare this young brother who was in such a favored position, seeing that he, himself was the natural heir to everything that was Jacob's? We don't really know the answer, but it is possible Reuben thought his father would hold him responsible for Joseph's safety. Also, we've seen already that Reuben had incurred his father's displeasure (35:22), so he may have thought his action in saving Joseph would put him back in Jacob's good graces.

Joseph's First Test

When Joseph came up to the group wearing his fancy robe, the brothers grabbed him, pulled off the robe and threw him in the well. Apparently, it was the dry season so there wasn't any water in it (37:23–24). It must have been nearly dark, for we are told that the brothers then sat down to have supper (37:25). Imagine what Joseph must have felt like at the bottom of this well, cold and alone in the dark and listening to his brothers' muffled conversation. For the first time in his life, he faced the harsh reality of suffering and death. Life had been an easy dream up to now, but suddenly it was a nightmare. We are not told if Joseph prayed, shouted curses at his

A view of Tell Dothan, a mound which marks the site of the ancient city. It was in this vicinity that the boy Joseph found his brothers, was thrown into the water well, and then sold to Midianite traders.

brothers, or tried in vain to climb out. But one thing is sure: Joseph could do nothing to save himself. Pleading, praying, cursing, or climbing all led to nothing but despair.

This was Joseph's first lesson in humility, a lesson he greatly needed to learn. If God had allowed this to happen, it was for Joseph's deeper transformation. Like coal miners who have been trapped by a cave-in, we too, sometimes find ourselves buried alive in a crisis where there seems to be no way out.

Just such a crisis once happened in my life. Late one night, a drunk driver ran my car off the road on a deserted stretch of highway. Like Joseph, I found myself trapped, in a ditch, in an overturned car, with no one around to help me. Death was very near as I realized that I could do nothing to free myself from the wrecked car. Eventually help did come, but the first moments of the crash and the feeling of total helplessness are forever burned into my memory. Sometime after that accident I began to realize that the reality of facing death had changed my view of life. Suddenly I was grateful for life itself, not just for what it gave me. And just as suddenly, I found myself aware of a God who was with me in *this* life, and not just in the next.

From Son To Slave

But, returning to Joseph, we are next told that Joseph's future took a new twist. Apparently Reuben had slipped away from camp, and while he was gone, the rest of the brothers spotted a caravan of traders coming down the road from Gilead on their way to Egypt (37:25). Judah suggests that these Ishmaelites–Midianites might be interested in buying a young slave for trade in Egypt. This way the brothers would not only avoid the responsibility for his death, but they would make a profit as well (37:26–27).

The caravan leaders were more than willing to co-operate with Judah's scheme. The deal was struck. Joseph was lifted out of the well, and sold to the Ishmaelite–Midianite traders for twenty pieces of silver (37:28). This was evidently the going price for a young male slave at that time (Lev. 27:5). Our story details are sketchy as to just how all of this worked out, but we are told that when Reuben returned to the camp and found Joseph gone, he was both furious and grief-stricken. His plan had backfired, and he felt that undoubtedly he would be blamed by his father for his young brother's loss. In apparent desperation he cries out, "The child is not; and I, whither shall I go?" (37:30). In all probability he is saying, "Where can I go to hide from my father's, and God's, anger?"

These words remind me of the feeling expressed by the Psalmist who saw so clearly that while we can be deceived, God cannot, "Whither shall I go from thy spirit? or whither shall I flee from thy presence?" (Psa. 139:7). Humankind has come a long way from Reuben's time around 1800 B.C. The intervening years have left us with countless examples of people who have served God faithfully and those who have tried to hide from God. But in reality, God is ever-present in our world. Neither the passage of time nor the breath-taking changes brought on by our late twentieth century technology can erase the truth that is deep down in us: We cannot escape responsibility for our actions and relationships, and we can neither ignore God nor hide from Him.

The Cruel Deception

To cover their tracks Joseph's brothers stoop to inflicting severe pain on their aged father as they kill a goat and splatter blood on Joseph's coat (37:31). Then they took the bloodstained coat to their father and had the gall to ask him if this was Joseph's coat. Of course it was, and they knew it. Jacob recognized it immediately, "It is my son's coat; an evil beast hath devoured him; Joseph is without doubt rent in pieces" (37:33). This was what they intended for him to think. Their lie and deception were complete.

Jacob's grief is painfully intense. According to the custom of the time he tears his clothes and puts on sackcloth as he mourns for his lost son over a period of many days (37:34). The rest of the family try to ease his pain, and his sons try to comfort him even as they hide the truth from him. Nothing seems to help as Jacob says, "I will go down into the grave unto my son mourning" (37:35).

Joseph's Silent Time

The closing sentence of Chapter 37 gives us a postscript about Joseph. We are told that the Ishmaelite traders sold him in Egypt to Potiphar, Pharaoh's security officer. Actually, Potiphar was the chief executioner. He was responsible for questioning, guarding, torturing prisoners, and for carrying out any death sentences that were ordered. In addition he also served as Pharaoh's personal bodyguard.

As Potiphar's slave, Joseph was probably responsible for all of the "dirty work" connected with running a prison. If so, his status was even lower than that of the prisoners, for he probably had to suffer their abuse and demands as he carried out his duties.

Joseph has come a long way from being the pampered son of a wealthy and aged father. Perhaps Jesus had Joseph in mind when he told the story of the Prodigal Son who also came from a good home but eventually found himself lower than the swine he was forced to feed (Luke 15:16).

Throughout this whole story of Joseph's ordeal at Dothan and his enslavement in Egypt, our storyteller has not given us one single word spoken by Joseph or any clue as to what he was feeling and thinking. Perhaps it is in this silence that he is learning to listen to God's voice and not just his own. A witty person once remarked, "God created us with two eyes and a mouth that will close and two ears that do not. Maybe this should tell us something."

Perhaps our writer intends for us to understand Joseph's silence as the silence of repentance. Later the Psalmist wrote words that might well have been spoken by Joseph, "I was dumb with silence, I held my peace, even from good; and my sorrow was stirred. . . . Lord, make me know mine end, and the measure of my days, what it is; that I may know how frail I am" (Psa. 39:2, 4).

It is quite likely Joseph learned a lesson in this period of silence that we twentieth-century children of God need to learn. Someone has said that we Christians are so busy broadcasting that we have no time or opportunity to receive. It is only as we actively listen to the voice of God that we become able to be effective witnesses.

Be Silent to God

Ours is indeed a noisy world. We are a supercharged society that runs with volume on full blast most of the time. We're uncomfortable when things get quiet. But it is only in the silence that we can hear the voice of God. There's an old Bulgarian proverb that says, "With silence one irritates the devil." Joseph had to have his time of silence, and so do we!

The words of Psalm 37:7 are quite familiar to us, "Rest in the Lord, and wait patiently for him." The literal Hebrew text reads, "Be silent to God, and let him mould thee." The picture is of a clay pot being shaped on the potter's wheel which must be centered so that it won't fly apart as it is being turned and moulded. Somewhere T. S. Eliot wrote that Christ "is the still point of the turning world." Well might we ask as we leave this part of our lesson, "What is the still point of my turning world?"

Judah and Tamar

In the next part of our Scripture lesson—Genesis 38—we leave the Joseph story temporarily for a rather earthy series of events that centers around Judah, one of Joseph's brothers. The story begins with Judah leaving home and going to live with his friend Hirah the Adullamite (38:1). Adullam was a city located about ten miles northwest of Hebron. Several centuries later this town gained some notoriety as the location for the cave which was David's hideout when King Saul was trying to kill him (1 Sam. 22:1). In addition to being one of Jacob's sons, Judah became an ancestor of both David and Jesus—as a direct result of the incidents which follow. So Judah is important to the story, and for awhile moves onto center stage. But like others whom God chose and used, he was a very human person who was more than a little capable of making some serious mistakes. Judah's first mistake was to marry a pagan Canaanite woman identified only as a daughter of Shuah (38:2).

She bore Judah three sons—Er, Onan, and Shelah (38:3–4). The storyteller compresses a lot of years into a few words, jumping from the boys' births to Judah's arranging for "a wife for Er his firstborn, whose name was Tamar" (38:6). And the only thing we know about Er is that he was a wicked man who died leaving Tamar childless (38:7).

Now, there was a custom that prevailed in the ancient Near East known as levirate marriage. Under this custom it was the duty of a brother-in-law to marry his brother's widow if the brother had died childless. The first son of this levirate marriage would be treated as if he were the dead man's son, and he would inherit all the dead man's property rights.

This custom didn't create undue complication during the times when polygamous marriage was permitted. However, in later societies where polygamy was not accepted, the brother-in-law, if he did not wish to take his dead brother's place, could decline after submitting to a specified ritual. The levirate marriage custom continued to be known throughout Old Testament times and was even referred to when certain religious leaders were challenging Jesus (Matt. 22:24).

So, in line with this custom, when Er died without a son, Judah instructed his next oldest son Onan to fulfill his duty to his dead brother by taking Tamar and getting her pregnant (38:8). For some reason, Onan refused to consummate his relationship with Tamar. According to the Genesis writer, Onan's refusal displeased the Lord and he died (38:10). This meant Tamar was still childless. Unfortunately, Judah's third son was too young to fulfill his duty to his sister-in-law, so Judah sent her home to her father's house to wait until Shelah grew up.

Several years later Judah's wife died. When the mourning time was over, he decided to visit his sheepshearers at Timnah, a town about ten miles west of Bethlehem (38:12). When Tamar heard of his plans, she removed her widow's garments, dressed up like a prostitute, and went out to sit on the side of the road Judah would be traveling. She had heard that Shelah was a grown man, but Judah hadn't done anything about their marriage. So, she plotted a bit of trickery to get back at Judah.

Right on cue, Judah comes along, sees the veiled "prostitute" by the side of the road, and makes it clear he wants to sleep with her (38:14–15). When she demands payment ahead of time, Judah offers to pay her in the future with a "kid from the flock." But Tamar isn't satisfied with this verbal promise because she didn't trust him, so she demands something as security. What would satisfy her? Judah asks, and Tamar demands his signet, his cord, and his staff. The signet was a ring worn on a cord around a man's neck which was used to stamp a man's "signature" or sign of ownership on important documents. In today's society it would be Judah's I.D. card.

Upon the satisfactory completion of this bit of sexual negotiation, Judah has intercourse with her.

Tamar Tricks Judah

Without knowing it, he is actually fulfilling the obligation owed by his sons. Having tricked her father-in-law Tamar returns to her own father's house and puts on her widow's clothing once again. (38:19). The storyteller makes no statement of approval or disapproval about Tamar's actions, but means to show how she will finally be given justice.

Later Judah sends his friend Hirah back to give "the prostitute" the promised kid from the flock, but she has now disappeared. Hirah is told by some men loitering around that the harlot has left; others say there never was a harlot at all. He reports all of this to Judah, who is obviously embarrassed by the whole incident, and says that he will just let her keep the signet and staff (38:20–23).

Tamar On Trial

When three months have passed, Judah hears that Tamar is pregnant. He self-righteously assumes that she has committed a sinful act, and orders that she be burned for dishonoring the family (38:24). Tamar, knowing that her life is at stake, sends word to Judah that she can identify the man who slept with her. In this ancient "paternity suit" Tamar produces the crucial evidence before Judah—the signet, the cord, and the staff (38:25). Although he knows that he has been tricked by Tamar, Judah admits that she has "been more righteous than I" because he had broken his promise to her, and he knew it (38:26).

Tamar had carried out a bold and risky plot to ensure that she would be given the children she was promised. In many ways she was a "sister" to Rebekah, who deceived Isaac for Jacob's sake, and to Rachel who deceived her father Laban, in taking the household gods, again for Jacob's sake. Both the men and the women in our Genesis story have been shown to be cagey and deceitful in their relationships with God and each other. And yet once again, in this tale of twists and turns, God's plan survives the wicked ways of people.

Tamar's Twins

When it came time for Tamar to give birth, we are told "twins were in her womb" (38:27). Then we have an uncanny replay of the birth of Jacob and Esau (38:27–30). The first born twin is named Pharez, from the Hebrew word meaning "to break out." The second son is named Zerah, which means "to appear."

Why is the birth of twins to Tamar so important? The story of Judah and Tamar's sons in this chapter will lead us to King David, who was born of their family line, through Pharez, Tamar's firstborn. The secret to understanding this family connection is found in the book of I Chronicles, where we learn that Boaz, Ruth's husband, was a descendant of Pharez (1 Chron. 2:5, 9–22). The son of Ruth and Boaz was Obed, David's grandfather (Ruth 4:18–22). And, of course, we know that Jesus would come through the family of Judah through David's line (Matt. 1:1).

Joseph, God's Hidden Treasure

As we return to the Joseph saga in Chapter 39, we are once again reminded by our storyteller that people who outwardly don't seem to have qualities of greatness often occupy a unique place in God's plan. In other words, to use an old cliché, you can't judge a book by its cover. As the Lord said to the prophet Samuel, when young David was designated as God's choice for king over his brothers, "For the Lord seeth not as man seeth; for man looketh on the outward appearance, but the Lord looketh on the heart" (1 Sam. 16:7).

Recently, I read a story about a man who saw a pile of rocks in a basket at a flea market sale. One of the rough stones seemed different to this rock collector. Taking a chance on a hunch, he bought the stone for five dollars. Later when he polished the stone, it was discovered to be one of the largest and most valuable sapphires ever found.

When we left young Joseph at the end of Genesis 37, there certainly was no indication he would ever become anything more than a miserable Hebrew slave in a harsh foreign land. But, as we pick up on the story again, we discover that a great deal has happened since Joseph was bought by Potiphar. The

A view of the Great Sphinx of Gizeh with the pyramid of Khufu in the background. The sphinx was a mystical beast in ancient Egypt and symbolized the Pharaoh in his role as Ra, the sun god. Sculpted out of natural rock, this sphinx, like most of them, had the head of a man and the body of a lion.

writer puts it this way, "And the Lord was with Joseph, and he was a prosperous man; and he was in the house of his master the Egyptian" (39:2).

Three Signs of God in Joseph's Life

In this part of our lesson now (Gen. 39) we will look at three events that show how God's claim on young Joseph became known to others: 1) in Joseph's success (39:1–6); 2) in Joseph's temptation (39:7–18); 3) in Joseph's imprisonment (39:19–23). Not only does Chapter 39 give us a great adventure story; it will also give us a chance to think about how God is with us in our success, in our hard decisions, and even in our suffering.

To set the stage for what is to happen we need to imagine what Joseph must have felt when he first arrived in Egypt and saw the wonders of that ancient culture. He certainly had never seen anything in Canaan like the pyramids and the palaces of the Pharaoh. He had been suddenly transported into a completely new and advanced culture.

Then, too, it may help us to understand parts of the Joseph story better if we have a little background on the Pharaohs who ruled Egypt during this period. Early in the eighteenth century B.C. Egypt was invaded and subjugated by an Asiatic people who were known as the Hyksos. This invading force was able to overrun the Egyptian armies readily because they had superior weaponry, including chariots drawn by fast horses—something unknown at that time in the Near East.

The Hyksos rulers replaced native Egyptian Pharaohs. They remained in power until around 1580 B.C. It is generally believed that their background was Semitic, which would have made them racially related to the Hebrew people and somewhat more sympathetic to them than the native Egyptians would have been. This could account in part for Joseph's ready acceptance first by Potiphar and later by the Pharaoh.

We've already been told that Joseph was sold to Potiphar. Now, some time after that original transaction, we read that Potiphar recognized that "the Lord was with him [Joseph], and that the Lord made all that he did to prosper in his hand" (39:3). You will recall that years before Laban saw some of those same qualities in Joseph's father Jacob (30:27).

God in Joseph's Success

Prosperity and privilege came to Joseph as he was appointed to the responsible post of overseer or administrator over the house of Potiphar (39:4). This meant that he didn't have to work in the fields or in the construction of tombs and public buildings as other foreign slaves were forced to do. Once again, we see that Joseph was given special advantages, and once again he lived the pampered life compared to the other slaves.

It has been said that the truest test of faith is not how we handle our pain, but how we handle our privileges. The last time Joseph enjoyed such a privileged life, he abused his position with arrogance and pride. In his father's house he had been a show-off and had turned his brothers against him. But in Potiphar's house, we begin to see a different, more mature person emerge.

In Potiphar's house Joseph was given charge over everything except the food, which could not be handled by foreigners for religious reasons. And, the writer says, "Joseph was a goodly person, and well-favored" (39:6). Other translations say that he was "handsome and good-looking," which may have also been true, but I like the King James translation because it shows us that he had a good heart and a good reputation, as well as good looks. Apparently Joseph had begun to learn from his exile and enslavement that greatness doesn't come from lording one's privileges over others, but from sharing the privilege of knowing the Lord.

The Bible continues to show us that true success does not come by right, by might, by birth, or by luck. Centuries later, when the Hebrew exiles returned from their captivity in Babylon, God revealed this same truth to their leader, the last king of David's line, Zerubbabel: "This is the word of the Lord unto Zerubbabel, saying, Not by might, nor by power, but by my spirit, saith the Lord" (Zech. 4:6).

One of the greatest leaders of our country was the son of a humble carpenter and suffered defeat after defeat in his early years. He lost races for the state assembly and the national Senate twice. He once said, "Let us have faith that right makes might, and in that faith let us to the end dare to do our duty as we understand it." Abraham Lincoln discovered this truth by overcoming defeat through faith in God's Spirit. Joseph will find this truth in his own life, discovering that as he loses his birthright—the power to control his life—God's Spirit will have the last word. What has the power to make our lives new again? Not our family or our fortune, but "my Spirit, says the Lord."

Humility and service has led to Joseph's success. Now these same qualities will be sorely tested in Joseph's great temptation. Just as his great-grandfather Abraham was put to the test, so God continued to polish Joseph's life by the same means.

Potiphar's wife apparently lived a life that was far more pampered than Joseph's. It is unlikely that she did anything worthwhile for others. Apparently her days were spent in being served and enjoying herself.

It is not surprising then that Potiphar's wife turned her lustful eye toward the young slave Joseph. "Lie with me," she demanded (39:7). Joseph refused her advances and reminded her that Potiphar trusted him and had been generous to him (39:8). Then Joseph openly acknowledged God's claim on his life. To break Potiphar's trust would also be a sin against God (39:9).

But Potiphar's wife continued to try to seduce Joseph, forcing him to avoid even being around her (39:9). Then came the fateful day when Joseph needed to be in Potiphar's house to conduct his business, and unfortunately, there was no one else around (39:11). This gave Potiphar's wife the opportunity she had been looking for. Grabbing Joseph's garment, she demanded that he have intercourse with her. But Joseph pulled away and ran, leaving his garment in her hand (39:12).

Now the rejected woman was really angry and lashed out in revenge. She apparently dashed outside and shouted out her lies about Joseph, accusing him of trying to seduce her (39:13—15).

When Potiphar returned home, his wife repeated her accusation and blames her husband for trusting this "Hebrew slave" in the first place (39:17)! Then, to prove her point she shows him Joseph's garment (39:18). Potiphar believes what he sees, and "his wrath was kindled" (39:19).

What do we carry away from this sorry scene? Perhaps we can see how much harm we do to others,

God in Joseph's Temptation

True Greatness

95

when we attempt to use them to get what we want. One of my favorite axioms is this: God created us to *use* things and to *love* people—not to *love* things and to *use* people. Joseph has learned not to use others, and now he has learned not to allow others to use him. Greatness does not come being gods, but from being God's.

God in Joseph's Suffering

Potiphar, outraged over what he thinks to be Joseph's betrayal of his trust, throws him into prison. Once again Joseph is betrayed and rejected (39:20) by everyone except God. But this time Joseph suffers because he has been faithful, and this marks him as a new man in God's eyes. Much later Jesus would say to His disciples, "Blessed are ye, when men shall revile you, and persecute you, and shall say all manner of evil against you falsely, for my sake. Rejoice, and be exceeding glad: for great is your reward in heaven" (Matt. 5:11–12).

The Lord Was with Joseph in Prison

Next, comes the good word as we read, "But the Lord was with Joseph, and shewed him mercy, and gave him favour in the sight of the keeper of the prison" (39:21). So even in an Egyptian prison Joseph is placed in a responsible position. For the third time in this story we see God reaching into every corner of the lives of those who follow Him. As He was with them, He is with us in our successes, in our temptations, and in our sufferings or failures.

A Christian Model

This truth should cause us to ask ourselves, "How do we find God in our own suffering?" I lost a very dear friend recently who used the last months of her life to bring *life* to others. When she learned several months before her death that her eighty-year-old heart was failing, she began to visit her loved ones and friends and gave away little treasures she had saved since childhood. She gave our young son her own childhood story books. And two weeks after her funeral, a package arrived for us which contained a gift she had ordered during the last days of her life. But most important of all, she had given us herself.

On the other hand, suffering can make us self-centered. If we let it, our pain can cause us to focus on ourselves and on our needs. But to endure suffering and face death without bitterness and selfishness is truly the mark of a fulfilled life. A life full of God's love has no need to fear want or suffering or even death.

The last verse in this part of our story tells us that "the keeper of the prison looked not to anything that was under his [Joseph's] hand" (39:23). This simply means that he trusted Joseph completely. To a visitor in that prison, Joseph would have in all probability looked like most of the other inmates, but the keeper knew there was something different about him.

My wife comes from a city in Michigan that is known for a particular stone. It is called the Petoskey stone. To see one of the stones lying on the ground wouldn't invite any particular attention. It is gray and dirty just like any other stone, but when it is polished by a jeweler or a trained rock hound, it takes on a brilliant beauty and reflects the marks of a master craftsman.

I believe it is something like this that the jail keeper saw in Joseph. He was different—God was with him. The jailer in Philippi saw that God was with Paul, his prisoner. And as a result, he became a believer in Jesus Christ (Acts 16:34).

We don't know what might have happened to Joseph's jailer. But we do know that he had the opportunity to see a great faith emerging from his humble prisoner as Joseph's life was being polished for even greater things to come. As we move on now to our next lesson we will learn how God's patient craftsmanship will reveal an amazing pattern and purpose in Joseph's life. And we, in turn, will find in this unusual man a model for our lives in this twentieth-century world.

God in the Pattern of Life

Lord God, you took the dungeon where Joseph was imprisoned and transformed it into a place of ministry and service. Help me to minister where I am, Lord. AMEN.

WHAT THIS SCRIPTURE MEANS TO ME
Genesis 37:1—39:23

Several years ago, I was doing some graduate work in Alexandria, Virginia. Shortly after the semester began, a faculty member asked if I'd be interested in doing some volunteer work with a member of his family who had multiple sclerosis.

Jeanne was confined to a wheelchair and had very little use of her hands. My duties would include lifting her out of the chair several times a day to help with her blood circulation. In addition I would prepare lunch for her twice each week.

Even though I felt good about my commitment to do this as a service project, I was terribly nervous at first. I had never been around anyone with MS, so I didn't know what to expect. I started my assignment with a lot of unanswered questions: What would we talk about? Would we like each other? What did she do to pass the time each day? How did she feel about herself and her physical condition? How would I respond if her physical pain caused her to have a crabby and negative disposition?

During the first few days, I merely performed the tasks I had agreed to do and didn't make any effort to promote conversation. It wasn't long, though, before I began to feel less nervous and much more comfortable with Jeanne. She always seemed so happy to see me, and she never complained, and always expressed appreciation for what I did. In spite of her physical condition and her total dependency on other people, she remained cheerful, polite, and seemed grateful to be alive.

My association with Jeanne lasted for three years, and I was constantly impressed and inspired by her inner strength, her positive attitude toward life, and her courage and determination to do the best she could with her limited physical abilities. And while Jeanne never spoke of her faith, her entire life was a visible witness of God's presence and love.

One small phrase in our Scripture lesson reminded me of my friend, Jeanne: "And his master saw that the Lord was with him . . ." (Gen. 39:3a). In order for Potiphar to have seen that the Lord was with Joseph, there must have been some visible evidence in his behavior that indicated God's presence. Perhaps he, like Jeanne, made the best of his present circumstances—remaining courteous and respectful, exhibiting a positive attitude in spite of the pain and suffering he had experienced. Perhaps he demonstrated a desire and determination to work to the best of his God-given potential. Perhaps he maintained a sense of inner peace in spite of conflict and disharmony in his family life.

We are not told what these "signs" were that caused Potiphar (and later, the keeper of the prison, Gen. 39:23) to see God's presence in Joseph's life. But we do know that his attitude and behavior were a visible witness of his faith.

It is my prayer that I will follow the examples set by Joseph, Jeanne, and countless others. May my daily actions speak clearly and boldly of my faith in God.

LESSON 5
GENESIS 40:1–42:38

God's Promise—
Joseph's Dream

Father God, Thank You for being faithful to Your promises. I appreciate You for using the detours and even the failures in my life to accomplish Your purposes. AMEN.

Joseph's rise to success in Potiphar's house was almost too good to be true. Who in their wildest dreams would have guessed that a Hebrew slave would almost immediately be in a position of respect and responsibility, working under an Egyptian official?

But now, at the very beginning of this lesson, we see that Joseph's life has become a nightmare. Unjustly accused by Potiphar's conniving and deceitful wife, he finds himself once again "at the bottom of a pit"—in a royal prison—with no hope of release.

Joseph and the King's Butler and Baker

Yet, as we discovered at the end of the last lesson, Joseph is still cast in the role of servant. But this time, instead of serving the noble family of Potiphar, he is serving two fellow prisoners who had incurred the personal anger of Pharaoh (40:1–4).

Perhaps some of Joseph's fellow prisoners were guilty of real crimes. Others, like Joseph, may have been innocent victims of someone else's deceit and were there through no fault of their own. Everyone in the prison, though, was suffering the same cruel fate—the loss of their freedom and the positions they had held on the outside. Having been sold into slavery from a secure and comfortable home and then falsely accused and thrown into prison, Joseph was in a unique position to understand and minister to others who had suffered failure and rejection as well.

A Christian pastor wrote recently about how to minister to families that are suffering grief. He said that somehow God uses the brokenness of our lives as bridges of understanding over which His love can move toward others. He further believes that the person who has had a significant loss can reach out to others as no one else can.

Recently, I was trying to comfort a young couple who had lost twin baby girls at birth. Someone reminded me that there was a wonderful support group of parents who had lost children in our town. I was given the name of one such couple to call. Then I was both amazed and humbled as I learned in talking with them that they, too, had lost twins and were most willing to help this grieving young couple in any way possible. They were indeed using the brokenness of their own lives as a bridge for God's love.

Joseph—a Bridge Builder

Joseph was about to become just such a bridge builder, first for some fellow prisoners and then for a nation, and finally for his own family. And his incredible comeback began with his insight into the inner life of two fellow prisoners, a butler and a baker, who "had offended their lord the king of Egypt" (40:1). Our storyteller doesn't say what offense they were charged with, but only that they were the victims of Pharaoh's anger and were thrown into prison with Joseph (40:2–3).

We are told that the captain of the guard entrusted Joseph with their care for some period of time (40:4). It is quite likely that during this time, Joseph may have shared his own story with the two men. And of one thing we can be sure, they had probably heard him speak of the Lord God whom he served. Perhaps they had asked this young Hebrew why his God had allowed him to succeed so greatly, only to fail so miserably. And perhaps Joseph had replied that his punishment came as a result of his faithfulness to God, and because of that he believed that God would deliver him as He had before.

A Night of Dreams

Next we are told that both the butler and the baker had a dream one night that troubled them (40:5). Then our storyteller gives us a clue as to what kind of person Joseph is becoming as he visits with the two men the next morning. Joseph was sensitive enough to recognize that something was wrong as he "looked upon them, and behold, they were sad" (40:6). It was obvious that both men were deeply troubled. And in response to Joseph's questioning they said they had each had a dream they couldn't understand (40:7–8). And with that Joseph tells them that his God is the interpreter of dreams, and he invites them to tell him their dreams (40:8). Actually, this is one of the few places in this complex tale where God is mentioned directly, but apparently the Genesis writer wants his readers to know that the interpretations will come from God and not from Joseph.

The Butler's Dream

The butler responds first and says that he remembers seeing a vine that had three branches that were loaded with ripe grapes. The butler said that he picked the grapes, pressed the juice from them into Pharaoh's cup, and gave it to him (40:10–11).

Then comes Joseph's interpretation, "The three branches are three days." Joseph goes on to tell him that in three days he will be freed from prison and restored to his former position as butler and cup-bearer for the king (40:12–13). With that came the wistful note as Joseph tells his butler friend to be sure to remember him and use his persuasive power to get his unjust sentence reversed (40:14).

And in a verse that is filled with emotion and longing Joseph reminds the butler that he "was stolen away out of the land of the Hebrews" and unjustly thrown into this dungeon (40:15). It is interesting to note that the Hebrew word for dungeon used here is the same word that was used for the pit where Joseph's brothers had dumped him (37:24). All of this reminds me of the words the Psalmist used about Joseph ". . . who was sold for a servant: Whose feet they hurt with fetters: he was laid in iron: Until the time that his word came: the word of the Lord tested him" (Psa. 105:17–19).

Now, as Joseph reflects on his lost home far away, he doubtless began to realize how much of his former life had been wasted in arrogance and ingratitude. Back then he had dreamed of his day of glory and triumph, but now he dreams of a day of mercy that will clear his name and give him a chance to begin his life again.

Centuries later the writer had this to say about King Hezekiah of Judah, "God left him, to try him, that he might know all that was in his heart" (2 Chron. 32:31). Without doubt Joseph was indeed going through a time of severe testing. We, too, experience those moments when it seems we are in "the pit" with no way of escape. Nothing reveals what is really in our hearts more than when we are left alone in the depths of trouble, and we must call on help that no human hand can give.

The Baker's Dream

Now we return to Pharaoh's second prisoner, the royal baker. The favorable interpretation of his butler friend's dream encouraged him to tell Joseph the content of his dream (40:16). This is his story, "I also was in my dream, and, behold, I had three white baskets on my head: And in the uppermost basket there was of all manner of bakemeats for Pharaoh; and the birds did eat them out of the basket upon my head" (40:16–17).

Again, Joseph responds immediately with an interpretation, but this time the dream's meaning spelled doom. The baker heard the dismal prediction: He would be hung in three days and his body would be devoured by preditors (40:18–19).

What Happened Next

Fortunately, the Genesis writer doesn't leave us in suspense long, for he immediately goes on to tell us that three days later Pharaoh celebrated his birthday and threw a big party for all of his servants (40:20). On the day of the party he restored his butler to his former place of honor and service and hung the baker just as Joseph had said (40:21–22).

But then comes the sad note. The butler forgot all about the Hebrew slave in the dungeon who had listened to him and offered him hope in his hour of trouble.

Joseph, Alone and Forgotten

Once again Joseph is alone—forgotten by the fellow-prisoner he had tried to help. Imagine, if you can, how he must have felt. These words of the Psalmist doubtless probe the depths of his feelings, "I am forgotten as a dead man out of mind: I am like a broken vessel" (Psa. 31:12). How often we've felt utterly alone and forgotten!

I've seen elderly people in nursing homes who have helped their children make their way in the world, but who are now forced to sit idly by day after day waiting for someone to remember them. This part of our lesson reminds us just how often we've been like the butler; we've forgotten those friends and loved ones who helped us along the way in bad times as well as good.

Pharaoh's Dream

Joseph languished in prison for two more years, seemingly completely forgotten, even by God. But next we're told that Pharaoh had a dream. He was standing by the great Nile River when he saw a strange sight. First he saw seven fat and sleek cows come up out of the river and feed on the grass along the bank—"in a meadow" (41:1–2).

As he continued to watch, he saw seven thin and scrawny cows come up out of the river. But then a strange thing happened. The thin, starving cows ate the seven fat cows. Strange! We'd say, "Weird." What did it mean? Especially since in those days cows were symbols of Egypt's fertility—much like the eagle is a symbol of America's strength.

That's the end of that scene along the banks of the Nile because we're told that Pharaoh awoke. But almost immediately we read that he fell asleep again and had a second dream. This time he saw seven ripe and plump ears of grain being swallowed up by seven thin and dry ears (41:5–7). Here was another weird and puzzling dream. No wonder Pharaoh's "spirit was troubled" when he woke up (41:8). As the supreme Egyptian god, Pharaoh needed to know what all of this meant, for he, like his countrymen, believed that dreams were important signs of the future.

Imagine his frustration, if you can, when none of the magicians and wise men in his court could interpret his dreams! Rephrasing the old nursery rhyme slightly, this was the situation: "All the king's horses and all the king's men couldn't put Pharaoh at ease again."

In the midst of this confusion the butler's memory is pricked. He remembers his young benefactor who is still in "the guard's house," and rehearses for Pharaoh all that happened to him when he was in prison (41:9–13).

Up from the Dungeon

In desperation Pharaoh is willing to try anything. So Joseph is released. He is shaved and bathed and dressed in clothing suitable for the Egyptian court, and he is brought in before the king. Then Pharaoh tells Joseph bluntly that he has had dreams that trouble him and no one knows what they mean (41:14–15).

Actually, this is rather a ludicrous scene. One of the mightiest heads of state in the world at that time reaches down and brings a young Hebrew slave not yet thirty years old out of the state prison into the splendor of his court and says in so many words, "I have heard of you. They tell me you can interpret dreams. Now, I need your help."

The old Joseph might have soaked up this flattery and said smugly, "That's what I've been trying to tell my dumb brothers for years." But this was a different Joseph. This was a Joseph who wasn't ready as so many of us are to believe our own press notices. Instead, he made it clear that while he didn't have the answers, God did! (41:16). It is dreadfully easy for us to take our abilities and gifts for granted, to begin to

Two views of the great pyramid of Khufu. By the time of Joseph, this pyramid was approximate 1,000 years old, having been built by King Khufu, the founder of the IV dynasty, who ruled Egypt around 2680 B.C.

believe that we are pretty good. As children of God, the Lord wants us to have proper self-esteem. But when we lose sight of the truth that it is God acting through us in grace, then life becomes a farce and all sense of meaning is lost.

The Joseph who stood boldly before mighty Pharaoh ready to listen to his dream had done a lot of growing up physically and spiritually since that day his brothers threw him into the empty water tank in Dothan. Joseph had come much further than merely the long miles that separated central Canaan from Pharaoh's court. Now, God was in charge.

Pharaoh's Dream and the Interpretation

Pharaoh launched immediately into a description of his dreams, and in doing so he tells Joseph that none of his court magicians and wise men had been able to interpret them (41:17–24). Then, just as soon as Pharaoh had stopped talking, Joseph spoke up and said, "The dream of Pharaoh is one: God hath shewed Pharaoh what he is about to do" (41:25). Imagine, if you can, the courage it must have taken for this young foreigner to stand before the supreme ruler and deity of the Egyptian civilization and tell him that the God of the Hebrews would determine his fate. But Joseph's was a God-given courage that is reserved for all of us who are faithful to our commitment as Christians.

Joseph told Pharaoh that the seven fat cows and the seven ripe ears mean the same thing—seven years of plenty for Egypt (41:26). Also, the seven thin cows and the seven bad ears mean the same—seven years of famine (41:27). Then to further authenticate the interpretation so Pharaoh would have no question as to the source of the revelation Joseph points to his God as the author of all that is to occur (41:28).

To make certain that Pharaoh understands what is about to happen Joseph makes it clear again that Egypt is about to experience seven years in which the crops will be good and there will be an abundance of food. And immediately following those seven good years will follow seven years of terrible drought and famine (41:29–31). And finally, Joseph says that the same message in two separate dreams is God's assurance that what is predicted will most surely happen (41:32).

Joseph's Plan for Egypt's Future

God never leaves us to confront difficult times without providing a way through. And this is exactly what comes next in our story. Joseph—the Hebrew slave whose recent home had been the Egyptian dungeon—then moves ahead boldly and gives the mighty Pharaoh a plan to save Egypt during the years of destructive famine. He suggests that Pharaoh appoint a wise and discreet man to manage the vast agricultural resources of the land during the seven years of bumper crops (41:33). Next, he advised Pharaoh to appoint regional officers who would carefully set aside and manage a fifth of all of the crops during the good years (41:34–36).

The Genesis writer now tells us that Joseph's plan was a hit with both Pharaoh and his advisers, and he immediately asks, "Can we find such a one as this is, a man in whom *the Spirit of God is?* (41:38, italics mine). Pharaoh's question doesn't necessarily signal the idea that he had become a believer, but it certainly tells us that he fully recognized that it was the Hebrew God who was responsible for what was happening.

This is only the second time the term, "Spirit of God" is found in the Book of Genesis. First, in Genesis 1:2 we're told that it was the Spirit of God that moved in creation bringing light and order to a dark and formless world. Now, here we get a picture of this same Spirit who is able to move into Joseph's darkness and Pharaoh's confusion and bring light and knowledge and understanding.

It is God's power and not our own that is the source of life and new life. In Genesis we see God's power both to create and to renew. The Psalmist said it well when he wrote, "Thou sendest forth thy spirit, they are created: and thou renewest the face of the earth" (Psa. 104:30).

Joseph's Rise to Glory

No sooner had Pharaoh asked "can we find such a one" than he came up with the logical answer. Since

Joseph had come up with the plan, he was the one to make it work. In just a few words, Joseph the slave was catapulted to the highest appointed office in Egypt. He was made Master of the Palace and Viceroy—second only to Pharaoh himself (41:40–41). Then, as a sign of Joseph's authority, Pharaoh takes the signet ring off his own finger, puts it on Joseph's finger, and then dresses him in the royal robes and jewelry that go with his new position (41:42).

There's something about this scene with Joseph in Pharaoh's court that is reminiscent of the Prodigal Son story when the son who had been hired out as a pig keeper was welcomed home by his father who " . . . said to his servants, Bring forth the best robe, and put it on him: and put a ring on his hand, and shoes on his feet" (Luke 15:22).

But Pharaoh wasn't through as he heaped another honor on young Joseph. In processions, Joseph's chariot would be number two—second only to Pharaoh's—and the people would be required to bow as it passed. And, finally, no official action could be taken in all of Egypt without Joseph's consent (41:43–44).

Then, to cap it all off Pharaoh makes Joseph a full citizen of Egypt by giving him an Egyptian name—Zaphenth-paneah, which means "code-breaker"—and an Egyptian wife, Asenath, the daughter of Potiphera (41:45). Potiphera was the Egyptian priest of On or Heliopolis, the center of sun worship in Egypt.

The Genesis writer dates Joseph's rise to power by telling us that he is thirty years old at the time (around the end of the seventeenth century B.C.). And now, after thirteen years of slavery and prison, Joseph is free to travel anywhere in the country as Pharaoh's number two man (41:46).

Before going on I want to insert a comment here. This event as it is told in our Genesis story is given historical authenticity not only by the biblical account but is also attested to by Egyptologists and archaeologists as being very realistic in terms of the customs of that time.

Outwardly an Egyptian—Still a Child of God

But back to Joseph now. It is important for us to remember that Joseph is married to the daughter of a pagan priest, and he is a ruler and leading citizen in a pagan society. He speaks the Egyptian language and dresses like an Egyptian nobleman. From all outward signs his Hebrew heritage has been set aside in favor of his newly acquired Egyptian status. But while people see only what is on the outside, God knows and understands the heart. Joseph's deep and abiding faith in his God is unchanged—as is his longing for his long lost family in far-away Canaan.

A very wise person worded it this way, "What matters about a man is not what lies behind him or before him, but within him." Soon Joseph will have the opportunity to reveal his true identity in God's own time and plan. The mark of true greatness is seen as a person through both good times and adversity holds steady to faith in the living Lord.

A minister friend of mine was once privileged to sit on a stage next to Mother Teresa of Calcutta. When she had completed her simple message, the audience burst into thunderous applause that lasted for more than twenty minutes. During that time my friend noticed that she just stood there motionless and with head bowed. She was completely still except her hands seemed to be fingering something.

Leaning forward so he could see her more clearly, he then realized that she was praying, totally withdrawn from what was happening with the crowd. Then he saw that she was fingering her rosary in deep communion with her Lord as if no one else was in the room. For my friend, this was the most electric moment of the whole evening. For it was her silence that revealed her heart, and her conquest of self was her greatest victory.

Joseph had conquered Egypt at age 30, but of far greater importance were his thirteen years of silence as a slave and prisoner, for it was then that he had conquered himself. This leads us to a couple of important questions. How do we tell the difference between what we are expected to be and who we are called to be? And, how do we conquer ourselves for God? As we examine Joseph's future years in these lessons, we will find a light that will show us the way.

Next, we are told that everything happened just the way Joseph, with the Lord's help, had predicted (41:47–57). There were "seven plenteous years" of abundant harvests. And during those years, Joseph, as Egypt's food controller, stored up vast amounts of food throughout the entire country, "And Joseph gathered corn as the sand of the sea, very much, until he left numbering; for it was without number" (41:49).

Joseph's Predictions Come True

We're told also that during these seven years two sons were born to Asenath and Joseph. The name of the first was Manasseh, which means in Hebrew, "Making to forget." Under God's guidance Joseph had been helped to forget his earlier hardship and any bad feelings he might have had toward his brothers (41:51). Joseph named his second son Ephraim, which means in Hebrew, "To be fruitful." Indeed God had turned Joseph's lean years into a fruitful time.

Then comes the next chapter in the dream saga. At the end of the seventh year of plenty our writer tells us that a destructive and crippling famine struck not only Egypt but all of the then-known world (41:53–54). When the private food supplies of the Egyptians were exhausted, we read that "the people cried to Pharaoh for bread: and Pharaoh said unto all the Egyptians, Go unto Joseph; what he saith to you, do" (41:55).

Pharaoh's words here remind me of some very similar wording that is found in the story of the wedding feast at Cana in Galilee. When Mary, the mother of Jesus, is told there is no more wine for the guests, she says to the servants of the host, "Whatever he [Jesus] saith to you, do it" (John 2:5).

In response to the food crisis we read that Joseph opened up the storehouses of grain so that everyone could have food (41:56). Joseph's actions here may indeed be symbolic in a way of what Jesus would do many centuries later. Jesus responded to the crisis of sin which afflicts the whole world by opening the storehouse of God's mercy and forgiveness so that everyone may come and receive grace and be saved from eternal death.

I like to think of God's love in the way the writer of one of my favorite hymns put it, "When through fiery trials thy pathway shall lie, my Grace all sufficient shall be thy supply." Even as we read that people from all over the world came to Joseph for grain (41:57), we should be aware that today there is a famine of peace and understanding afflicting the world and a spiritual hunger that only One can satisfy. As Joseph became the one source of food at that time, so Jesus is the one source of Life for every person. Indeed, our instructions in responding to the needs of our neighbors nearby and across the world are reminiscent of these words, "Whatever he saith to you, do it."

Jacob Sends His Sons to Egypt

In the spring of 1987 news spread like wild fire that United States Savings Bonds could be bought at a generous interest rate for only two more days. Record crowds flocked to banks across the country for this "last chance" sale. This certainly goes to prove that good news travels almost as fast as bad. When Jacob heard the good news that there was grain in Egypt, he evidently acted quickly so his starving family could get their share. For all he knew this was their "last chance." So now our storyteller says that Jacob turned to his sons and said in effect, "Why do you stand there frozen like statues?" (42:1). Somehow I get a picture here of men just sitting around in despair waiting for and expecting the worst.

There have been times when I've driven along a back country highway at night and have spotted a rabbit in the road ahead. Sometimes they just seem to freeze in fear instead of jumping out of the way. I have a feeling in this scene that Joseph's brothers were something like those scared rabbits who had to be jolted by Jacob's sharp words.

When he's got their attention, Jacob tells his sons that he's heard there is food in Egypt, and he instructs all of them except young Benjamin to go and buy grain for their survival (42:2–3). It is obvious that Jacob still smarts and is grieving from the loss of Joseph many years before as he refuses to let Benjamin go "lest peradventure mischief befall him" (42:4).

The Dramatic Meeting

In obedience to their father's instructions the ten brothers make the long and hot trip south and west to Egypt to "buy corn" (42:5). Then as our story unravels we discover that Joseph has so much control over the grain distribution that even common buyers went to him. And it is quite likely that foreign buyers were checked out especially well.

Among the foreign buyers on one particular day were the ten sons of Jacob who "Bowed down themselves before him [Joseph] with their faces to the earth" (42:6). They didn't recognize this austere Egyptian official, but we're told that Joseph recognized his brothers immediately.

Next, we discover that Joseph hasn't forgotten his boyhood dream in which his brothers' bundles of grain bowed down before his (42:9). Now those same brothers are bowing low before him. What irony!

From the description of this first meeting between Joseph and his brothers he assumes a severe posture and avoids letting them know that he understands their Hebrew language. Instead he talks to them through an interpreter and accuses them of being foreign spies who are just pretending to be grain buyers (42:9).

This accusation quite likely strikes terror into the hearts of the brothers, and they protest by saying they have only come to buy food and they are all honorable sons of one man (42:10–11).

Joseph pretends this doesn't satisfy him, and he again charges them with being spies who have come to check out conditions in Egypt. In desperation now Jacob's sons respond, *"Thy servants* are twelve brethren, the sons of one man in the land of Canaan; and, behold, the youngest is this day with our father, and one is not" (42:13, italics mine).

In this exchange Joseph undoubtedly learned a

great deal about his brothers. It is even possible he felt a little sense satisfaction when he heard them refer to themselves as "thy servants." At the same time, though, he got the message that they remembered their "lost" brother. This was just the confession he had been waiting for, and now he begins to bait the trap that will catch the brothers in their guilt.

Joseph's Brothers Are Tested

Joseph continues to be adamant, "Ye are spies." Then he puts them to the supreme test. Refusing to believe them he says that nine of them must remain in Egypt while one brother returns to Canaan and brings the young brother back to Egypt. Only by doing this can they prove their truthfulness! Then he puts all of them in prison for three days where they would have plenty of "think time." Those had to be three long days for the agonizing brothers (42:13–17).

At the end of the third day Joseph had the ten men brought back before him. This time, though, he offers them an easier test as he says, "This do, and live; for *I fear God*" (42:18, italics mine)—here we have the first clue to his identity as he admits to his reverence for God.

Then Joseph goes on to give them a new option: One brother must remain behind as a hostage while the other nine return for their young brother (42:19–20). Now, the Genesis writer takes us behind the scene and we are given the opportunity to listen in on the brothers' conversation among themselves.

They immediately relate all that is happening to them now with what they had done to Joseph many years before. Their feelings of guilt have cut deep crevices in their souls over the years, and they see themselves being punished for their evil actions (42:21–22).

The brothers, of course, were talking among themselves in Hebrew quite sure no one would understand them. But Joseph heard their confession of guilt and was deeply moved. In part, they had passed Joseph's test, but he still has Simeon, the second oldest brother, retained as a hostage (42:24).

The brothers are now free to return home with the

grain Joseph has ordered put in their sacks. But Joseph had surreptitiously instructed those helping
him to put the brothers' money in the sacks as well.
This was his little surprise that would only be discovered when the brothers were well on their way or
had arrived home. And so with a full load of grain
they leave Egypt for their father's home in Canaan
(42:25–26).

The Awful Discovery and the Trip Home

Imagine the shock when one of the brothers opens
a sack at an inn stop along the way and discovers the
money (42:27). When he tells the others what has
happened, they are all terror-stricken, and again,
their guilty consciences interpret this as a judgment
from God. From this we see that they had known all
along they had sinned not only against their brother,
but against God as well.

This is a fact of life that has been a part of our
human condition since the beginning of time. Then
Jesus affirmed the principle in His parable of the last
judgment when in speaking of the failure to help
others He said, "Inasmuch as ye did it not to one of
the least of these, ye did it not to me" (Matt. 25:45).
From this we have come to understand that to injure
a brother, to wrong a neighbor, to deprive other people of what is rightfully theirs, is to sin against God.

The brothers hurry straight home, and the next
scene has them telling their father everything that
has happened to them. They rehearse the entire
scene and wind up with the Egyptian's insistence
that their young brother accompany them back to
Egypt (42:29–34). Then to add to their fear, each
brother discovers his money as he opens the sacks.
And probably one of the great understatements of
the whole story comes right here as the writer says,
"They were afraid."

At this point old Jacob's despair peaks, and he
lashes out at his sons, "Me have ye bereaved of my
children: Joseph is not, and Simeon is not, and ye will
take Benjamin away: all these things are against me"
(42:36).

Even though Reuben tries to reassure his father,
Jacob is adamant. Benjamin, his only other son by his

Darkness Before the Dawn

beloved Rachel, shall not go. Jacob is a broken man with no confidence in the future (42:37–38).

As we come to the end of this lesson, we are left at a very dark stage of our story. There seems to be absolutely no hope, no way out. Everything is lost. But to leave it there is to leave out God.

Recently, I was deeply touched by a news story that told of the tragic circumstances surrounding a family of seven brothers, the oldest of whom was 19. Their mother had died, their father had abandoned them, and their home had burned to the ground. By court order the boys were split up and sent to different foster homes. But then a miraculous series of events occurred.

The oldest boy petitioned the court for custody of his younger brothers and won back all but the two youngest. Then as the case was made public, donations of money poured in, and a house and small farm was given to them. With all of this outpouring of love and resources, the brothers were all reunited again.

Those boys had experienced, as had Jacob's sons, a terrible time of darkness and suffering, a time when their family was all torn apart. But God is always to be reckoned with. His plan for their lives and ours cannot be defeated by a Potiphar or a butler or a baker or even a Pharaoh.

I believe the Genesis writer means to give us a story of a creation that is wrecked by human sin but is renewed by God's love. The darkness of our present lesson is like the darkness and void that covered the earth moments before God said, "Let there be light." It is like the darkness of Joseph's years in prison before he was released. And now, as we journey together in our study of God's Word, let us see not only the darkness but the promise of the dawn.

Lord Father, Thank You for renewing me day by day with Your love and Your mercies, which are new every morning. AMEN.

WHAT THIS SCRIPTURE MEANS TO ME
Genesis 40:1—42:38

Within walking distance of our house is a small neighborhood park. Our two-year-old son, Brian, enjoys going there to swing, pick wildflowers, explore in the woods, and play on the gate leading to the tennis courts.

Frequently, we will then walk across the field to the Viking Hills Elementary School where there is a covered cemented area that always captures Brian's attention. He follows the painted lines of the running lanes, knocks on the basement doors, makes funny noises and listens for his echo, and identifies each number as he steps on the squares of the hopscotch boards. I'm sure he thinks of this as his own private playground! Then when Brian begins to get restless with his play routine, he will invariably head toward the back of the school where there are several steps and a ramp leading up to the office entrance.

It is at this point that my protective, motherly instincts switch into high gear! I automatically reach for Brian's hands to steady him as we climb from the steps up to the top of the ramp. Then I hold his hand tight as we run full speed down the ramp.

When we first began this little exercise, Brian was content to let me help him. But now, he's more independent. He wants to climb up himself, and he refuses my attempts to help him. But once he turns around at the top and begins picking up speed on his descent, he insists that I help him keep his balance.

In this lesson, we read of the butler and baker who offended the Pharaoh in some way (Gen. 40:1). Because of their offense, they were put in prison and remained in the custody of Joseph. While in prison, both the butler and the baker had dreams that Joseph later interpreted. After telling the butler that he would soon be restored to his former position, Joseph says, "But think on me when it shall be well with thee, and shew kindness, I pray thee, unto me and make mention of me unto Pharaoh, and bring me out of this house" (Gen. 40:14). A little later, though, we read that when the butler was released from prison and was back in Pharaoh's service, he forgot all about Joseph.

This reminds me of the attitude that some people have toward God. When life seems to be going well, and they feel in control of the situations around them, they tend to become quite independent. They often ignore God's presence, or drift away from Him. No longer is any effort made to maintain a close, personal relationship with God through prayer, worship, or fellowship with other Christians.

But then, when the pace of life increases dramatically, or circumstances get out of control, these same people turn to God for help, guidance, direction, strength, and protection. Like Brian, they grab for a steady hand only when they can't maintain their balance by themselves. They welcome God's help when they are in danger, but forget Him when things are going well.

I've heard it said that affliction is the shepherd dog God uses to drive us back into the fold. Sometimes it takes suffering or adversity to make us realize our need for God's strong embrace. Certainly, He is always present to comfort and uphold us during these difficult times. But we are really cheating ourselves if we turn to God only when we're faced with conflict or strife. As we develop a strong, personal relationship with God, He will enrich our lives and give us the kind of faith and trust that will be with us every moment of the day.

LESSON 6
GENESIS 43:1–45:28

Jacob's Family Reunited

Heavenly Father, Help me to surrender my fears and defenses to You. My security doesn't depend on whether or not there is a famine in the land. You are my only assurance of provision and safety. AMEN.

As our narrative continues now at the beginning of this lesson, we are reminded that "the famine was sore in the land" (43:1). There was no letup, and this simply meant that as soon as the grain ran out for Jacob's clan, the brothers would have to return to Egypt for more supplies. But we left our last lesson with Jacob absolutely refusing to send Benjamin with them as the Egyptian viceroy had demanded. It also meant that all during this time Simeon, Jacob's second son by Leah, was languishing alone in the Egyptian prison.

Once again we see that Jacob, who had been forgiven by his brother Esau, refused to forgive his own sons. And those sons were still unable to confess their guilt about Joseph. All of this simply meant that the famine in Jacob's house was not only physical but spiritual as well.

About a year ago I learned that a father's love

A Bitter Family Quarrel

means far more than just supplying food for the family. During the time that my little son was just learning to talk, I was terribly busy and didn't arrive home at night until way past his bedtime. But he had learned to say "bye-bye" to me as I rushed out the door in the morning.

After several weeks of having only a few hurried moments with my son in the morning, I planned to take a whole day off to spend with him. As I eagerly went into his bedroom that morning, he was lying very still, just looking up at me. As I reached down to pick him up, he said, "Bye-bye, papa." Tears welled up in my eyes as I realized that I had given my son everything he needed except me. Later, a friend who heard me tell this said, "Sometimes others can fill in for you at work. No one can fill in for you at home."

Just providing food for the table wasn't enough for my family, and it certainly wasn't enough for Jacob's either. Although they didn't know it at the time, God was planning a big change for Jacob's clan, but nothing could happen until they confronted their need for more grain.

Eventually, that day came. The drought continued in Canaan. There were no crops and they were running out of corn. Jacob told his sons, "Go again, buy us a little food" (43:2). It was just a simple and cryptic command. Our writer doesn't tell us whether Jacob said anything about Simeon in the Egyptian jail or about the Egyptian ruler's request to bring Benjamin. Had Jacob accidently or purposely forgotten these important details? We don't know.

We do know, though, that Jacob's sons hadn't forgotten because just as soon as they were told to go back and buy corn, Judah reminded his father that the Egyptian food administrator had said, "Ye shall not see my face, except your brother be with you" (43:3). And that started a family quarrel.

Judah laid down the law. They will go if Benjamin goes with them, but if Jacob refuses, they won't go. Then to make sure his father understands, Judah repeats the demand that was made if they were to get more food from Egypt (43:4–5).

Jacob-Israel is very disturbed by the situation and lashes out at his sons for even mentioning they had a younger brother at home. Obviously, at this point the attack is irrational—most quarrels are. Defensively the brothers respond by saying something like this, "How were we supposed to know that he was going to ask us to bring Benjamin back with us?" (43:7).

A Solution Offered

Apparently Judah knows that now is the time to press an advantage. Enough has been said; it is a decision that is needed. First, he reminds his father that if they and Benjamin don't go after food all of their children will starve. Then he offers to be surety for Benjamin—he will personally be responsible for his young brother's safety and will guarantee his return (43:8–9).

Jacob's Bitter Choice

Jacob now understands that the only way he can hope to save Benjamin is by giving him up, for to keep him at home is to condemn him to certain death by starvation. But to let him go would be to give him a chance to live, even if he never returned to Canaan. Many years before, Jacob's mother, Rebekah, had faced the same awful decision. When Jacob's life was threatened by Esau, the only way Rebekah could save her favorite son was to send him away (27:42–43).

One of the hard lessons for us to learn is that God may at times keep from us certain things we desperately want so that we will remember He is really the only thing we can't live without. In Francis Thompson's well-known poem "The Hound of Heaven" a man finally comes to see why God has not given him everything he wanted. In poetic language the author has God asking the man, "Who else but God would love you just as you are?" Then Thompson has God continue with these words,

"All which I took from thee I did but take,
Not for thy harms,
But just that thou might'st seek it in My arms.
All which thy child's mistake fancies as lost,

I have stored for thee at home.
Rise, clasp my hand, and come!"

Jesus worded it this way, "But seek ye first the kingdom of God . . . and all these things shall be added unto you" (Matt. 6:33).

Judah's arguments and his personal pledge force Jacob to realize that he can't have everything his own way. If his family is to survive, he must concede to the demands of the Egyptian official. So he tells his sons to prepare for the return trip to Egypt. In an effort to win the favor of the mysterious Egyptian viceroy Jacob tells his sons to take him a personal gift of spices, resin, balsam, almonds, pistachio nuts, and honey—all Canaanite delicacies. They were, of course, to take money to pay for the corn plus the money they had found in their bags on the previous trip home. And, finally, they were to take young Benjamin (43:11–13).

Nothing But God's Mercy

Jacob's final act before his sons leave was to pray, "And God Almighty give you mercy before the man, that he may send away your other brother, and Benjamin" (43:14). This is the first time the Genesis writer speaks of Jacob mentioning God's name since Rachel's death. It would appear that Jacob's loss of both Rachel and Joseph had turned him into a bitter and disappointed man. But now in the desperation of this moment he says, "If I be bereaved of my children, I am bereaved." In other words Jacob has reached the place of total dependency on God; there is no way for him to save his family except by God's mercy.

When we confront the reality that our only hope for living and experiencing a rich and full life rests in God's mercy, we have seen the truth—about God and ourselves. It is when we admit that we have reached the limits of our own strength and wisdom that God's infinite wisdom and strength can turn our insurmountable obstacles into steppingstones that lead us into His great new society, the kingdom of God.

I recall so well that when I lost my first job after

college, I was convinced my world had ended. I just knew my future was destroyed because no one would ever want to hire a laboratory technician who had failed at his first job. I felt rejected and was bitter.

But then came a call from the supervisor of a laboratory in another city. I learned that he had hired a technician friend of mine who had also been fired from the lab where I had worked. She had turned into a successful employee, and now he was offering me a job as well.

I asked him why he was willing to give me, an unknown, another chance. I'll never forget his reply, "Look, I believe that young people are a lot like young trees. Sometimes the right tree is planted in the wrong soil and is unable to grow. Sometimes people, like trees, need a chance to grow in a different environment before they can bear fruit."

Later I learned that this man had a deep Christian faith—one which had been tested by his own failures—failures that had become steppingstones to God's mercy. Now he was showing me the same mercy he had received, and by doing so he gave me more than a job. He gave me the opportunity to wipe out the bitterness I was feeling about the past so I could grow again and bear fruit. Reflecting on this episode in my life helps me identify closely with Jacob at this point.

Jacob's Sons Return to Egypt

Once again Jacob's sons start south on the caravan route to Egypt. Jacob is left alone just as he was that night on the banks of the Jabbok River—alone, except for God. At that moment he was unable to look into the future and see how God would transplant him and his family from the famine-parched soil of Canaan with its bitterness and regret to the lush richness of Egypt's delta and its peace and renewal.

But before this undreamed-of change in Jacob's family could take place, his sons would have to come face to face with their lost brother and discover how God makes what is broken whole again. As their father had wrestled with the angel on the river bank, they would have to "wrestle" with their own consciences and discover as their brother Joseph had that their future would not be decided by their own efforts but by God's grace.

The Dramatic Meeting

In a very few words our Scripture writer moves Jacob's sons from southern Canaan to Joseph's headquarters in Egypt. Imagine, if you can, their anxiety, the tightness in their chests as they face the unknown. Then imagine Joseph's feelings as he sees his younger brother—the only other son of his own mother.

Our only clue as to Joseph's emotions at this point comes as he turns aside to his steward and instructs him to take the brothers to his house where they would be his guests at the noon meal. The brothers hadn't been able to understand Joseph's instructions, so when they were led to Joseph's house, they were sure some kind of a trap was being set for them. Immediately they moved into a string of explanations about what had happened to them on their last trip, how they had discovered the money in their grain sacks but had now brought it back with them (43:20–22).

A Puzzling Reassurance

When they had run out of explanations, the brothers heard some reassuring but puzzling words from Joseph's steward, "Peace be to you, fear not: your God, and the God of your father, hath given you treasure in your sacks: I had your money" (43:23). Then he brought Simeon out to them. I'm sure their minds were a whirl as they wondered how this Egyptian knew about their God. And why would their God give them a treasure they hadn't earned or even deserved?

Then, too, why were they being treated like guests instead of criminals? (43:24–25). There was something strange going on, and as we would put it today, they were waiting for the other shoe to drop.

Joseph Takes Charge

As soon as Joseph arrives home, the brothers attempt to give him the personal gifts they had brought for him. But he doesn't appear to be particularly interested either in the gifts or their bowing and scraping. Instead he inquires immediately about their father—is he still alive? Is he in good health? I'm sure Joseph is hoping that he isn't too late—that Jacob had died without knowing that his lost son was alive and well in Egypt.

I'm reminded here of Dickens' famous character, Scrooge, who finally goes out into the street after a long and fearful night. Then he nearly scares the wits out of a small boy when he barges up to him and asks, "Boy, what day is it?" When he is told it is Christmas Day, Scrooge is immensely relieved because it isn't too late for him to become a new person and begin again.

Now Joseph learns that he isn't too late. His father is still alive and well (43:28). Then, looking around the room he sees Benjamin and asks, "Is this your younger brother, of whom ye spake unto me?" And not waiting for a response, Joseph adds, "God be gracious unto thee, my son" (43:29). Once again, Joseph has planted a clue as to his identity, for this salute to Benjamin was common in Canaan and in the Near East but was quite unknown in Egypt.

Next comes one of the most touching scenes in our Old Testament Scriptures (43:30). Seeing his younger brother was too much for him, and his emotions boiled over. Joseph had to leave the room for a time in order to regain control.

Joseph Dines with His Unsuspecting Brothers

After Joseph pulled himself together he washed his face, returned to the dining hall, and gave instructions for the meal to begin. Our writer gives us a parenthesis here by inserting the word that while they all ate in the same room, Joseph and his brothers did not eat at the same table "because the Egyptians might not eat bread with the Hebrews" (43:32). According to the custom of that time, a special table was set up for Joseph that faced his brothers. This didn't necessarily have anything to do with rank. Rather, there was a great difference of opinion between the Hebrews and Egyptians as to what was suitable to eat—what was "clean" and what was "unclean." So it is quite likely that different food was served and this required their sitting at different tables.

Next comes another interesting fact. As the brothers looked around at their table, they realized that each was sitting according to his rank—his age. How did their host know to seat them this way? From Reuben to Benjamin, each was properly placed. But then as the food was brought in, Benjamin received five times more than each of the others. Even this little bit of trivia has its purpose. It was customary in those times for a king to be served twice as much food as anyone else at his table. But Benjamin's allotment seems to indicate that his host felt he was worth more than two kings.

Undoubtedly, under other conditions the brothers would have wondered why the youngest was treated the best. But they had gone to Egypt expecting the worst, and all they could do now was marvel at the kind and generous treatment they were receiving. And with that, they settled down and "drank, and were merry with him [Joseph]" (43:33–34).

Joseph's Final Test

As our story moves along now, Joseph is instructing his servants to fill up his brothers' sacks with grain so they can be loaded onto the pack animals for the long trip back to Canaan. But then he appears to be up to his old tricks again as he instructs his steward to "put every man's money in his sack's mouth" (44:1). But this time something else is added, "And put my cup, the silver cup, in the sack's mouth of the youngest" along with his corn money (44:2). This was apparently a special cup that Joseph used for drinking, but it was also the kind of cup that the magicians and soothsayers used to read omens—sort of an Egyptian crystal ball. At any rate, it was likely the brothers had seen Joseph using it when they were dining at his house, so they would recognize it immediately.

When the loading process was all completed in the early morning, the brothers hurried on their way with a great sense of relief over the success of their trip. But before they had gone very far Joseph instructs his steward to chase after them and accuse them of betraying him by returning evil for the good he had done them (44:4–5).

A view of the Avenue of the Rams at the Temple at Karnak. Karnak is located on the Nile River in central Egypt. Building techniques were wonderfully sophisticated in ancient Egypt.

The steward carries out his master's plan right on cue. He intercepts them and accuses them of wrongdoing. But the brothers protested their innocence by saying that if anyone of their group had stolen anything, he should be killed and the rest of them consigned to a life of slavery (44:6–10).

The steward, though, insisted that their judgment was too severe and said that the guilty party would become a slave but everyone else could go free (44:10). Then the brothers unloaded their sacks and examined them all beginning with Reuben. To their horror the silver cup was found in Benjamin's sack (44:12).

Now comes the great test. According to the steward's terms only Benjamin would be taken prisoner; the rest were free to go on home to Canaan. Would the brothers abandon young Benjamin as they had once abandoned Joseph? Have the recent years worked a change in their hearts to where they would risk their own lives to save Jacob's last favorite son?

The brothers' next move gives us the answer to these questions. Without hesitation everyone of them reloaded their pack animals "and returned to the city" (44:13). There they were confronted by the brother they hadn't recognized and who accused them of their wrongdoing.

Judah's Confession and Plea

Following the short but pointed accusation that Joseph levels at his brothers, Judah launches into a lengthy and passionate rehearsal of all that has gone on since the famine struck Canaan (44:16–34). This is a deeply moving part of the story as Judah reminds the Egyptian ruler of their aged father who had already lost one son, and now to lose another one would be more than he could handle.

Judah then tells how his father was persuaded to let Benjamin come this time because he had offered to be personally responsible for the boy's safety and certain return. Then comes the clincher, "Now therefore, I pray thee, let thy servant abide instead of the lad a bondman to my lord: and let the lad go with his brethren." In other words Judah is saying, "Keep me as your slave and let my young brother go home to our father." There is just no way Judah could stand to see his father again unless Benjamin was with him (44:32–34).

Joseph's Answer, and God's

In this passionate plea of Judah's and in the united front of the brothers Joseph could see the incredible change that had taken place in their lives. They had passed the test. Sometimes the greatest gift that we can offer God is being honest with Him. It is then that God can respond to our need as we admit the truth about ourselves—that we are powerless to help ourselves and that we've not shown the same degree of mercy to others that we want for ourselves. When we reveal our true selves to Him, we discover God's true self—He is the One who sees who and what we truly are and loves us anyway.

I once heard author Keith Miller tell the moving story of a young nun who went to her bishop to report that she had seen a vision of the Lord. The bishop decided to put the young woman to a test. He told her that the next time she had a vision of the Lord, she should ask Him to tell her the answer to this question, "What was the bishop's sin before he became a bishop?"

A few weeks later the young nun returned to the bishop's office and reported that once again she had seen the Lord. Without hesitation the bishop inquired as to whether she had asked the Lord the question. She admitted she had, and he then asked impatiently, "What did the Lord say?"

After a brief silence the young woman looked up and said that He had answered, "I don't remember." This fits in with the comment an unidentified person once made, "Pardon, not wrath, is God's best attribute."

The young woman in Keith Miller's story passed the bishop's test by revealing that God had truly forgiven him. Judah and his brothers had passed Joseph's test by revealing that God had really changed their lives. Now Joseph had nothing left to hold against them, for if God had refused to abandon them in their sin, he could not either.

Joseph Reveals the Secret

We now move rapidly to the emotional climax of this story. As Judah concluded his speech, we can be sure the brothers were watching the Egyptian's face closely in an effort to read what he was thinking. Then they watch as he instructs all of his personal and household attendants to leave the room. The atmosphere must have been wrapped in tension as the frightened Hebrews waited to see what would happen next (45:1).

Expecting his rage and vengeance, they see instead his tears. Joseph's release of his long-held-in emotions was so loud that even the servants heard it from behind closed doors (45:2). Today people of Near Eastern descent are still quite emotional in their outbursts of both joy and sorrow. And in that setting Joseph makes his surprise announcement, "I am Joseph." They were startled and didn't seem to comprehend. Is it any wonder?

Then our writer gives us this scene as Joseph says, "Come near to me I pray you. And they came near. And he said, I am Joseph your brother, whom ye sold into Egypt" (45:3–4). Now they understood. After all, only Joseph himself would have known that they had sold him to Ishmaelite-Midianite traders many years before. They were terror stricken. They were face to face with the brother they had wronged, but now he was Pharaoh's own second in command—a mighty man in a great country.

Doubtless, seeing the terror on their face, Joseph immediately gives them unexpected assurance, "Now therefore be not grieved, nor angry with yourselves, that ye sold me hither: for God did send me before you to preserve life" (45:5). In other words, he is now telling them not to be afraid. In spite of evil intentions God's plans and purposes were working out. No longer must they feel guilty and blame themselves—all is forgiven.

Joseph's model at this point is hard to follow. No, it is impossible to follow without the grace of God at work in our lives; we just can't do it on our own. But with His help we must. Holding grudges, being critical of our fellow Christians, undercutting the actions and reputations of others are corrosive and cancerous. Only God's grace can bring healing and the ability to love and accept others as daughters and sons of God.

Joseph's Plan for the Future

Now Joseph tells his dumbstruck brothers that his being in Egypt was God's doing and not theirs, ". . . he [God] hath made me a father to Pharaoh, and lord of all his house, and a ruler throughout all the land of Egypt" (45:8). He had been placed by God in a position to help people everywhere to have food during these years of severe famine.

Next, Joseph tells his brothers that there will be five more years of drought and famine. The only way they can survive is to return to Canaan, get their father and the rest of his clan, and return to Egypt and settle in the land of Goshen where they and their herds and flocks can live in peace and plenty. There he can look after them and care for them (45:9–11).

At this time in Egyptian history it was not uncommon for the Pharaoh to grant sanctuary to foreign nomads. And during the rule of the Hyksos, who were themselves of Near Eastern origin, the eastern part of the Nile Delta was often a haven for troubled and needy foreigners.

The Reconciliation Is Complete

Now that the truth is out, Joseph and his youngest brother embrace and weep for joy. And with that, the spirit of reconciliation is shared among all of the brothers. They kiss each other and cry together and "after that his brethren talked with him" (45:14–15). What a beautiful thing! Now that the obstacles among them were all gone, they could *really talk with each other.* This is a need we all have—to be able to communicate with persons who care is one of our greatest joys.

When Pharaoh heard about this glad reunion, we read that he was pleased. In fact, he fell right in line with Joseph's plan. He instructed Joseph to provide his brothers with wagons and supplies so that the move of Jacob's clan from Hebron to the land of Goshen would be as easy and comfortable as possible (45:16–20).

We're next told that Joseph acted on Pharaoh's instruction—wagons, changes of clothes, money, and vast supplies of food were all given to the brothers. The caravan that moved out of Egypt toward Hebron in southern Canaan had to have been an impressive sight. To the happy brothers that two hundred miles must have seemed much easier than before. They were anxious to reach their father and tell him the good news.

Jacob Learns the Truth

When the caravan arrived at Jacob's encampment in Hebron, he was given the good news that Joseph was alive and that it was he who was "governor over all the land of Egypt" (45:26). The old man's reaction could be expected—his "heart fainted, for he believed them not." We have virtually no details as to what happened next. Possibly the brothers made a full confession to their father as to what they had done with Joseph. Possibly when Jacob learned how Joseph had forgiven his brothers, he was able to forgive them too.

But whatever happened, as Jacob heard more about Joseph and as he saw the wagons and supplies that had made the trip from Egypt—he believed. In fact, our writer says, "The spirit of Jacob their father revived." I'll bet it did! Now he had something to live for. His words were pregnant with emotion, "It is enough; Joseph my son is yet alive: I will go and see him before I die" (45:28).

God's Extraordinary Use of Ordinary People

It has been said that the story of Joseph can only be truly interpreted when we see that God is the main character. But we, who witness these events in Genesis, do not always see who their true author is. For as Joseph was not recognized by his own brothers, God is sometimes not recognized in the events of the lives of His own people. For even in the Bible, God does not always act in spectacular or miraculous ways. Rather, He often chooses to act unrecognized, through ordinary events and ordinary people—events and people that we *can* recognize. Often the events and the people God uses are not "holy." The Bible never tries to hide the weaknesses of the people God calls to serve Him. Nor does the Bible tell us that innocent people never suffer the "terrible slings and arrows of outrageous fortune," as Shakespeare's Hamlet once said.

God used the brothers' jealousy to get Joseph to Egypt. He used the spitefulness of Potiphar's wife to get Joseph in touch with Pharaoh's butler, who recognizes his extraordinary gift. He used Pharaoh's inexplicable dream to bring Joseph to Pharaoh and to power in Egypt. Then He used a family's need for food to bring that family back together again. And He used even Joseph's deception to reveal his brothers' repentance, so that an old wound could finally be healed.

In other words, God can use our weaknesses as well as our strengths to accomplish His purposes in the world. And He takes events that seem to be certain catastrophe and redeems them completely. Jacob could never have imagined how the sacrifice of his beloved son would bring redemption to his whole family.

Many years ago in college, I had two friends who seemed to have terrible handicaps. One was totally blind and the other was completely paralyzed from the waist down. But they were both graduate students who had applied the gifts that God had given them to overcome obstacles that most of us never dream of. And one of the greatest of these gifts was their friendship.

Both of them loved ice cream, and I often saw them heading across campus toward the ice cream shop. The blind young man would push the wheelchair of the paraplegic friend, who would use his eyes to direct them both! Sometimes when we cannot see the way, or when we have a hard time moving in the direction we want to go, God doesn't always explain why. But our limitations can be occasions for His strength, just as we have seen in the story of Joseph, and in the story of my two college friends.

Our Father, Your strength is revealed in my weakness. You show Yourself to be dependable and effective in every situation. AMEN.

WHAT THIS SCRIPTURE MEANS TO ME
Genesis 43:1—45:28

In order to earn extra money while in graduate school, I did a lot of babysitting. Occasionally I stayed with children for several days while their parents went away on vacations or on business trips. Most of the time I enjoyed this contact with children, and I especially appreciated the opportunity to escape dormitory life for a while.

However, one such child-care arrangement proved to be a disaster. I had agreed to stay with a fourteen-year-old girl for one week. My responsibilities included driving her to and from school, fixing meals, watering the many plants in the house, and feeding and walking the dog. Wendy's parents explained that she was quite independent, but they wanted me there to provide some company for her and to make sure that everything went smoothly.

On Friday afternoon, I drove up to the junior high school just as Wendy was coming out the front door. She had a sour expression on her face as she slammed the car door and snarled, *"Don't* ask me how my day went!" Since I decided not to try and make conversation, we maintained a cool silence all the way home.

Shortly before dinner, Wendy informed me that she needed to go to the store. Having anticipated my resistance, she explained, "I need toothpaste, deoderant, and stuff like that." I thought this was rather strange, but since her parents had left money for food, gas, or whatever we needed, I gave in to her demand.

I waited in the car while Wendy went into the store. She soon returned carrying a grocery bag full of small boxes and containers—toothpaste, shampoo, deoderant, soap, suntan lotion, chips, soda, cereal, and trail mix. Since she was in such a disagreeable mood, I didn't ask her why she needed all those things, but I certainly wondered what was going through her mind.

After gulping down her dinner, Wendy told me she had to clean the basement and garage. This, too, seemed odd. Most of the teenagers I knew weren't especially anxious to clean anywhere. "Don't wait up for me to finish," she said as she flounced down the stairs. "I don't need a *baby*-sitter."

Early the next morning, I heard a loud truck engine in the driveway, followed by the sound of the garage door slamming. I got to the window just in time to see Wendy thrust a loaded backpack into the pickup and climb into the cab. She and her male friend were gone before I could get to the front door.

When I thought back on the events and comments of the night before, I realized just how oblivious I had been to her signals. Wendy's attitude, actions, and nasty remarks had all been signs indicating her intention to run away. And even though I was puzzled by her behavior, I had neglected to question her or confront her in any way.

I think Joseph's brothers were just as oblivious to the signals coming from the "Egyptian" food administrator. They failed to pay attention to his frequent questions and curiosity concerning their father and younger brother (43:27, 29). Joseph's blessing to Benjamin (43:29) went unnoticed. And they didn't respond to Joseph's unusual behavior when he rushed to his chamber to cry (43:30). Then, too, they weren't the least suspicious when Benjamin was served extra food (43:34).

There has been an important message for me in this lesson. I hope that I can benefit from my own experience with Wendy and that of Joseph's brothers by learning to pay closer attention to the signals of those around me. It is important for all of us to become more aware of those signals that might indicate trouble spots: a sad tone of voice, unusual behavior, negative attitudes, sudden changes in mood, etc.

May God give us the ability to see and listen with our hearts as well as with our eyes and ears. Then, I pray that he will give us the strength and courage to respond to human needs in faith and love.

LESSON 7
GENESIS 46:1–47:31

"Jacob's Last Journey"

---

*Lord, Help me to glean the truths You have for me in this lesson.
Amen.*

The Lonely Pilgrimage of Age

I know from experience with many families that it is very hard for elderly persons to have to pack up their belongings, leave their own home and move to another city where their children live. To be torn between the love of one's children and the love of one's home is a terrible dilemma. A great-aunt of mine lives alone in a house that was her parents' home. All of the family in her hometown are gone now. And my great-aunt's children live so far away that frequent visits are not possible. In a recent Christmas card, she admitted to struggling with the decision of whether to sell her home or try to find a live-in companion.

On the one hand there are the loneliness and the memories that fill the quiet house, as the poet Thomas Moore described it in his poem "Oft in the Stilly Night":

Like leaves in wintry weather,
　　I feel like one
　　Who treads alone,

Some banquet-hall deserted,
Whose lights are fled,
   Whose garlands dead,
    And all but he departed!

On the other hand there is the fear of living, and worse, maybe dying in a strange place. An English soldier, William Hodgson, later killed in France during the first World War, once wrote:

I, that on my familiar hill
Saw with uncomprehending eyes
A hundred of thy sunsets spill
Their fresh and sanguine sacrifice,
Ere the sun swings his noonday sword
Must say goodbye to all of this
By all delights, that I shall miss,
Help me to die, O Lord.

Jacob Looks Back in Beersheba

As we begin our seventh lesson, we find old Jacob confronted with deciding whether to stay in familiar Hebron or go to Egypt. At last, he has regained his lost son Joseph, and he desperately wants to be with him. He has said, "I will go," so, with the decision made, he first travels south to Beersheba, the southernmost city in Israel, on the trade route to Egypt.

It was at Beersheba where his grandfather Abraham had dug a well. It was the place where his father Isaac had offered sacrifices to God. And it was here that Jacob had once lived before he set out for Haran to find Laban (28:10). So many important things had happened in Jacob's life in Beersheba, it seems natural that he would come here to pray to his father's God (46:1).

Many years earlier, God had spoken to Jacob in a dream and promised him, "Behold, I am with thee, and will keep thee in all places whither thou goest, and will bring thee again unto this land; for I will not leave thee, until I have done that which I have spoken to thee of" (28:15). Now once again, God speaks to Jacob in the "visions of the night," calling him by name, "Jacob, Jacob." And Jacob answers, "Here am I" (46:2).

137

God's Promise for the Future

Then Jacob receives these marvelously reassuring words from God, "I am God, the God of thy father: fear not to go down into Egypt; for I will there make of thee a great nation: I will go down with thee into Egypt; and I will also surely bring thee up again: and Joseph shall put his hand upon [close] thine eyes" (46:3–4).

Most certainly, with the promise that there was nothing to fear and that God would be with him, Jacob could feel that he had a new lease on life. Then, the latter part of God's promise can be interpreted in one of two ways. First, even though he will die in Egypt—where his son Joseph will close his eyes in death—his final resting place will not be there. Or this part of the promise may refer to future generations of Hebrews who would one day return from Egypt to the land of promise.

In future studies we will discover that both interpretations of that promise were eventually fulfilled. But the important thing for us to understand here is that there was more involved than a family reunion, as important as that was. The stay of Jacob's family in Egypt was a part of God's great plan for his descendants, for from them He would shape a great nation.

The promise of God's presence in verses 3 and 4 is renewed again and again in Scripture—for all of us. The hymnwriter Richard Keen put the promise this way in a much-loved hymn;

Fear not, I am with thee, O be not dismayed!
For I am thy God, and will still give thee aid;
I'll strengthen thee, help thee, and cause thee to stand,
Upheld by my righteous, omnipotent hand.

As believers in Him, we can trust God in all times and in all places, because whenever and wherever we go, He is with us.

In reflecting further on God's reassuring words to Jacob in verses 3 and 4, we are reminded that for all the Patriarchs, in spite of their terribly human lapses at times, God was always their hero. He was the center of their thinking and of their story. It is true, of course, that their understanding of God became much clearer with the passing years. In contrast to their pagan neighbors who worshiped hostile gods that demanded child sacrifice, the God of Abraham, Isaac, and Jacob was a friendly God who cared deeply about them and promised to be with them.

Jacob Finds His Lost Son

With God's reassurance Jacob is ready to go to Egypt. He no longer has any doubts. The assembling and packing process begins, and the wagons Joseph sent are loaded with the household belongings of this large family. It is no small thing to move a family of three or four, let alone one as large as Jacob's had become (46:5–7). The scene must have been one of pandemonium—crying babies, eager children, reluctant and complaining teenagers, shouting, crying, the noise and bleating of large herds of animals.

I'm sure that many times during this process mothers and fathers were taking headcounts to make sure all of the children were there and ready. Accounting for everyone was also apparently very important to the Genesis writer, because now he lists in careful detail the names of all of Jacob's children and their children (46:8–25). The total of Jacob's clan who settled in Egypt, including Joseph and his sons, was seventy people (46:26–27).

As the caravan moves closer to the Egyptian border, Jacob sends Judah on ahead to let Joseph know they are coming and to get directions to the place where they were to settle—the land of Goshen (46:28). In an intensely moving scene, Joseph himself takes to his chariot and rushes out to meet his father. After believing for nearly twenty-five years that Joseph was dead, so overwhelmed is Jacob in being reunited with his long lost son that he exclaims, "Now let me die, since I have seen thy face, because thou art yet alive" (46:30).

I've often wondered if Luke wasn't thinking of this touching scene as he described the joy of old Simeon when he held the baby Jesus in his arms in the temple. He had longed all his life for a glimpse of God's redemptive plan, and when he realized who the babe was, he, like Jacob, could now anticipate a peaceful death: "Lord, now lettest thou thy servant depart in peace, according to thy word: For mine eyes have seen thy salvation, Which thou hast prepared before the face of all people" (Luke 2:29–31).

Jacob's New Outlook

Since Joseph's disappearance (37:33–35) it seems that Jacob has been filled with thoughts of bitterness and death. How tragic it is when with the passing years people become obsessed with the past and focus on what they've lost or what has changed rather than on what was gained. With Jacob now this has changed. He has a renewed hope for the future. Peace displaces bitterness and disappointment in the heart of the old Patriarch.

A wonderful prayer about growing old, written by an anonymous author, goes like this,

God keep my heart attuned to laughter
When youth is done;
When all the gray days, coming after
The warmth, the sun.
God keep me then from bitterness, from grieving,
When life seems cold;
God keep me always loving and believing
When I grow old.

Not everyone will find again the people and the things that have been lost in the past as Jacob did. But the words of this prayer hold a promise that we needn't lose the ability to laugh, to love, and to believe if we trust in God, whose love endures forever.

A Place for Strangers

Joseph knows that it would never work for his aged father and nomadic family to try to settle in one of the Egyptian cities. For one thing, they would feel the same discomfort that all country people do in a crowded cosmopolitan city. Then, too, Joseph knows that the Egyptian city people don't want to be close to wandering shepherds and would much prefer they live in a part of the country away from the cities (46:34b). So now he takes steps to be sure that Pharaoh will really accept them and give them wide open spaces for their herds and cattle.

Joseph tells his family that he will go and report their arrival, and he will remind Pharaoh that they are wandering shepherds from Canaan so he will agree to their settling in a place suitable to their life-style. In the meantime Joseph has carefully coached his family on how to respond to Pharaoh so things will work out according to plan (46:31–34). Of utmost importance was the need to emphasize their vocation, "Thy servants' trade hath been about cattle from our youth" and to remind Pharaoh they know "every shepherd is an abomination unto the Egyptians."

Joseph has grown quite clever in dealing with the Egyptians. If his family puts themselves down, he knows they will most likely be assured of living a separate and segregated life from the Egyptians. This would mean a minimum of intermingling and inter-marriage and would help preserve their Hebrew life-style in this foreign country.

Pharaoh Meets Joseph's Family

So Joseph carries out this plan. He first goes to Pharaoh to tell him that his family and their herds have arrived, and for now they are staying in Goshen (47:1). Then he presents five of his brothers to Pharaoh (47:2). Undoubtedly, he selected five that he felt would make the best impression!

Almost as if on cue, Pharaoh asks, "What is your occupation?" And the brothers respond by saying they are shepherds as their ancestors were (47:3), and they ask Pharaoh to allow them room to pasture their flocks in Goshen (47:4).

In response, Pharaoh turns to Joseph and grants permission for Jacob's family to settle permanently in Goshen. He even adds that if there are any men of "activity" (not lazy!) among them, he will allow them to herd the royal cattle (47:5–6).

Next, Joseph brings in his father and presents him to Pharaoh. Jacob apparently wasn't overly awed by the ruler and human god of the Egyptians. We are told that Jacob blesses Pharaoh, rather than the other way around (47:7). Possibly recognizing a patriarch

If measured from its most remote headwaters, the Nile is the longest river in the world, and from the earliest of times it has figured prominently in Egypt's history. It was in the Nile Delta in lower Egypt where Jacob's family settled in Goshen. Joseph and his brothers would have known the Nile well.

of much greater age than himself, Pharaoh asks Jacob, "How old art thou? (47:8).

Jacob's answer is full of the wit and irony of an old man telling his story to a younger one. He has been a pilgrim for 130 years, Jacob says. He wants to impress Pharaoh that he has been around a long time and has seen many places and knows a lot about human nature. This, of course, establishes him as a sage or a wise man. And then, warming up to his tale, old Jacob says that "few and evil" are the days of the years of his life. By this he means that he has lived a very long time, but that his years are brief and futile compared to those of his ancestors (47:9). Finally, Jacob once again gives Pharaoh a blessing, and then he tells him goodbye (47:10).

I find a delightful irony in the fact that these "abominable shepherds" end up with some of Egypt's most prime acreage, and their father, a wandering herdsman, blesses the lord of the Egyptian empire. Of course, behind the humor, there is, once again, clear evidence of God's hand in the episode. Our storyteller is showing us that God can use anybody to accomplish His will. He can "put down the mighty from their seats," and exalt "them of low degree" (Luke 1:52). All of this reminds me of the story of the English shrimp peddler who was ordered out of the way by a member of Parliament when he was trying to park his limousine. "Look out yourself," the peddler shouted back as the official honked his horn again. The driver then leaned out the window and said, "Do you realize that I have an M. P. at the end of my name?" Without a moment's hesitation the peddler snapped back, "So 'as every blarsted shrimp in this 'ere cart!"

A Homeland for the Humble

After getting his family nicely settled in the rich Goshen area of the Nile delta (47:11–12), Joseph is now confronted with a new crisis. As the terrible famine persisted, the Egyptians for the most part had used up all of their money reserves in buying grain. Now, broke and hungry, they came to Joseph. "Give us bread: for why should we die in thy presence?" they demanded (47:15).

Joseph's New Famine Plan

In response to this desperate need Joseph decided to accept cattle in exchange for grain and food and so for all of that year the people traded every kind of cattle for food (47:16–17). But when the Egyptians ran out of animals, they were again in a desperate condition. Since they had nothing else to barter with, they offered themselves and their land to Pharaoh in exchange for food. This simply means that in order to stay alive, the people became slaves to Pharaoh. Only the priests, who were still offered a food allowance, avoided this servitude (47:18–22).

Finally, we are told that Joseph devised a plan for the slaves' survival whereby he would supply them with seed. It could be planted on Pharaoh's ground so that when crops were again harvested, they would have grain. In exchange they were required to give one-fifth of it to Pharaoh as a tax. Four-fifths of their harvest could be retained for their own use (47:23–24).

Joseph's measures seem extremely harsh to us, because we're unfamiliar with the customs of ancient Egypt. In those days the people were used to autocratic forms of rule and considered slavery to Pharaoh better than death. The important thing is that Joseph can be credited with preventing general starvation even as he kept the country from going bankrupt.

The People Are Thankful

Even in the face of unimaginable hardship and the loss of everything, our writer tells us that the people were thankful just for being alive. They showed their gratitude to Joseph by saying, "Thou hast saved our lives: let us find grace in the sight of my lord" (47:25).

In ministering to people who have faced great hardships, or experienced severe accidents or losses, I have sometimes found that the only thing they could be truly grateful for is what *didn't* happen. I have also come to feel that we could all use more of what a minister friend of mine calls an "attitude of gratitude"—an attitude that is thankful for both what has happened to us and what hasn't happened to us. The orthodox Jews have a saying that we should be able to give thanks for everything. For instance, when a brick falls off a building and hits us on a foot, we should stop and thank God—that it didn't fall on our head!

Apparently the people of Egypt learned to express gratitude for the four-fifths of their harvest that they got to keep rather than complaining and begrudging Pharaoh the one-fifth they had to pay him (47:26). Like Jacob, their days had become "few and evil," but they were still thankful for what they had.

I remember so well an elderly lady I used to visit who had lost most of her hearing and was terribly crippled with arthritis. I felt very sorry for her, but I discovered that she had a more positive attitude about her disabilities than I did. She said to me one day, "Maybe my senses ain't too good, but I still got good sense."

Jacob "Leans" on Faith

The scene shifts quickly now from the difficulties of the Egyptians to Jacob's family and their life in Goshen (47:27). The picture we get here is that they used their resources well and prospered. The Genesis writer says, "They had possessions . . . and grew, and multiplied exceedingly." The last seventeen years of Jacob's life in this fertile country near his son Joseph were undoubtedly happy. He lived a total of 147 years—long enough to see the beginnings of the fulfillment of the promise God had made to his fathers and to him.

When Jacob knew that his death was near, he called Joseph to his side for one last request. God had promised him a land to call his own, and he knew that promise couldn't be fulfilled in Egypt. His request was simple: He didn't want to be buried permanently in Egypt. And so he said, " . . . Thou shalt carry me out of Egypt, and bury me in their [his fathers'] buryingplace" (47:30). This Joseph promised to do. Now Jacob could rest in peace. His wrestling with himself, with his family, and with his God was nearly at an end. The last verse in our Scripture lesson says that "Israel [Jacob] bowed himself upon the bed's head" (47:31). To "bow oneself" meant to pray.

But the same Hebrew word used for "bed" in this verse could also read "staff." To say that Jacob *leaned on his staff* gives us a powerful symbol of his lifelong pilgrimage. Years before when Jacob had been faced with the awful fear of crossing the river to meet his brother Esau, he had bowed his head in humility to God and prayed, "O God of my father Abraham and God of my father Isaac, the Lord which saidst unto me, Return unto thy country, and to thy kindred, and I will deal well with thee: I am not worthy of the least of all the mercies, and of all the truth, which thou hast shewed unto thy servant; for with *my staff* I passed over this Jordan; and now I am become two bands" (32:9–10, italics mine).

Jacob's journey was a pilgrimage toward faith. His

own schemes never led him into a life of security and promise. Only the faith of the Psalmist who leaned on God's Word and said, "Yea, though I walk through the valley of the shadow of death, I will fear no evil: for thou art with me; thy rod and thy staff they comfort me" would sustain Jacob.

Many years later the writer of the Book of Hebrews looked back on Jacob's pilgrimage in this same way, "By faith Jacob, when he was a dying . . . worshipped, leaning upon the *top of his staff*" (Heb. 11:21, italics mine).

The Shepherd's Staff

The shepherd in ancient Israel grasped his long staff in the center. He used it not only for climbing hills but also for beating the brush for snakes, and for guiding sheep. The staff was the shepherd's most important tool, for it could be used to support him, defend him, and direct his flock in the proper way.

As Christians we have a staff to carry all the way through life. We have God's promise that He, the great Shepherd, will support us, defend us, and lead us in His way. As Jacob leaned on his staff through his life, so should we in our own pilgrimage take nothing but the staff of Christ and lean on Him and His presence with us.

Our seventh lesson has for the most part been centered on Jacob's old age. I would like to close it with a story from the last days of our sixth president, John Quincy Adams. His words to an old friend who passed him on the street speak quite well of the peace that is ageless and the faith which always sustains the heart even when the body is spent and bent with age.

Mr. Adams was making his way feebly down a Boston street when an old friend stopped him and, grasping the trembling hand, asked, "And how is John Quincy Adams today?"

"Thank you," said the ex-President, "John Quincy Adams is well, I thank you. But the house in which he lives at present is becoming quite delapidated. It is tottering on its foundations. Time and the seasons have nearly destroyed it. Its roof is pretty well worn out. Its walls are shattered, and it trembles with every wind. This old tenement is becoming almost uninhabitable, and I think John Quincy Adams will have to move out of it soon. But he himself is quite well, quite well."

To be quite old and yet to be quite well in one's heart can only happen as we look forward, not into darkness but into the Light of God's presence. That Light is the promise of Jacob. It is the gateway to heaven that is open for us in the One who still says, "I am the way, the truth, and the life: no man cometh unto the Father, but by me" (John 14:6).

Father God, Help me to lean on You. Sometimes it's tempting to take so-called control of things—to rely on my own resources. Help me to lean instead on Your "everlasting arms." AMEN.

WHAT THIS SCRIPTURE MEANS TO ME
Genesis 46:1—47:26

As I began reading this lesson, a question arose in my mind, "Do many people actually read through the entire list of names found in Genesis 46?" My tendency is to skim through such lists, or to skip them completely. Of what interest or value is a list of names? For the most part, these children, who were descendants of Jacob, are mentioned only one time in the entire Old Testament. And here, they're not even noted for their accomplishments or contributions. Their names appear only because of their relationship to Jacob.

Seeing this list of names caused me to recall an incident which occurred when I was a student at a community college in Michigan. During the two years there, I was involved in numerous school and extracurricular activities: journalism, intramural sports, the student senate, and the social planning committee.

In my sophomore year, I received a letter stating that my name had been nominated to appear in the forthcoming edition of a national publication recognizing junior college students. This was quite an honor, and I felt really proud of myself at the time. I appreciated the fact that my scholastic achievements and extracurricular contributions had been noticed by the faculty and administration. It was a pleasure to fill out the enclosed application form reciting the leadership positions I had held as well as the various degrees, honors, or awards I had received.

Several weeks after completing and mailing the necessary application I received another letter from the board of this publication. It informed me that volumes containing lists and brief biographical summaries of each nominee would soon be available for purchase. These deluxe editions, with luxurious heirloom bindings and gold embossed pages would become lasting tributes to those people whose names were selected to appear. Another special remembrance, a personalized paperweight, was also offered.

Both of these memorials seemed extremely expensive and were totally outside the constraints of my personal budget. At the time, I was greatly disappointed that I couldn't afford the book or the paperweight. After all, being nominated and accepted into this organization was an honor which I had earned. It irritated me to think that I would have no tangible evidence of this award.

Hindsight has helped me to see this incident more clearly. I was placing more importance on the material items than on the recognition. I should have gained a great deal of personal satisfaction just knowing that I was included in that group of outstanding junior college students. That was a lasting tribute in itself. No tangible evidence could or would add any further significance to the honor.

Looking back at this incident I realize that my view of honors and awards has completely changed. Lists of my personal accomplishments and contributions are no longer important to me. I don't particularly care whether or not my name appears in a book or if I am awarded any medals, plaques, or certificates. What matters is the sense of fulfillment I receive when I'm working to achieve personal goals.

We are not always rewarded in this life for the things we do. Sometimes the only satisfaction we receive comes from within. But for me, that inner pride and joy far outweighs the spoken or written praise and recognition from others.

LESSON 8
GENESIS 48:1–50:26

Free at Last

Lord, You have already made me free in Christ Jesus—free from the world's values and methods. Help me to walk daily in that freedom. AMEN.

As long as I live I will never forget the Christmas Eve twenty years ago when my father took my brother and me to visit our grandfather for the last time. As each of us held one of his hands, he spoke his last words to us—words that burned deeply into our consciousness and have enriched and shaped our lives ever since.

Our grandfather was a plainspoken, no-nonsense man from New Hampshire who loved his life's work and his family. He wanted very much to leave behind something of value for his present and future family. But as I think back now, I know that he gave us something on that Christmas Eve that was far more valuable than any material bequest. He gave us his blessing. Among other things he told us, "Live your lives so that when it comes your turn to die, you can say that the world is a better place for your having lived here."

Our lesson opens with Jacob on his deathbed. The aged Patriarch knows the time is short, so he sees to it that word gets to Joseph (48:1). We are privileged to become a part of this emotional scene as the Genesis writer tells us that Joseph takes his two sons, Manasseh and Ephraim, to the bedside of his dying father.

Word of their coming reached Jacob, and he was up and ready for them when they arrived (48:2). As we would expect under such circumstances, Jacob opened the conversation by looking back over the long years to the time the Lord had met him at Luz (Beth-el) and had blessed him (28:13, 19). It was there God had promised that his family would be "fruitful and multiply" and that one day they would possess the land God had promised to his grandfather Abraham (48:3–4).

For Joseph, his father's acceptance of his sons and his blessing upon them was very important. After all, they were half Egyptian. Would they be accepted to participate in God's promise? Could they be a part of Abraham's legacy? Would they be committed to the God of Abraham rather than to the gods of Egypt?

But if such questions flooded Joseph's mind, he was quickly reassured. Without hesitation Jacob gives Manasseh and Ephraim an equal place in his family with his other sons—he literally adopts Joseph's sons as his own. But more than that, he insures their descendants a place of equality in the generations to come. Now, Manasseh and Ephraim are not just grandsons of Jacob, they are sons as well. This touching scene reminds me of the saying that "God has no grandchildren, only sons and daughters."

As Jacob continued to reminisce, He looked back to that sad day when his beloved Rachel, Joseph's mother, died and he buried her at Bethlehem (48:7). Little did Jacob know that one day at Bethlehem, a baby would be born that would take God's blessing to all the children of the world. While the old Patri-

Jacob Blesses Joseph's Sons

Jacob's Past and Promise

arch couldn't see down the future of his family line, he trusted in God's promise that out of the sadness of a burial at Bethlehem would come a new birth of hope and joy.

Evidently, at this point Joseph had moved his two sons forward right in front of his father. Like his father before him, Jacob was too blind to see or recognize the boys so Joseph had to identify them (48:8–10). As he does, Joseph puts Manasseh, the oldest, at Jacob's right hand and Ephraim at his left. Joseph intended for the oldest to have the favored place.

It was a common practice in ancient Israel for fathers to bring their children to great men of faith for their blessing. Our counterpart of this today is always a glad occasion when we take our little ones to the house of God where they receive the blessing of a clergyperson in the name of the Lord. In this service we are doing what the mothers did when they brought children to Jesus, "And he took them up in his arms, put his hands upon them, and blessed them" (Mark 10:16).

Jacob's Surprise

Now, with the two boys standing at each knee, carefully positioned by their father, Jacob makes a surprise move. He crosses his arms so that his right hand is resting on the head of the younger son and his left hand is resting on the head of the oldest son. Before blessing them, however, Jacob first pronounces a blessing on Joseph. Then he adds, "The Angel which redeemed me from all evil, bless the lads; and let my name be named on them, and the name of my fathers Abraham and Isaac, and let them grow into a multitude in the midst of the earth" (48:16).

While this was going on Joseph made an attempt to reposition his father's hands (48:17–18). But Jacob refuses, saying in effect, "I know what I'm doing." Then he adds that the descendants of both young men will be great but Ephraim's will be greater (48:19–20). Indeed, their descendants occupied a place of prominence especially during the period of the judges and the monarchy.

The blessing being given to the younger son is reminiscent of what happened between Jacob and his brother Esau. This time, though, the scene is free from the deception that had caused Isaac, who was also blind, to give the younger Jacob his blessing instead of Esau. Jacob knows what he is doing and why. And we're told that the nation of Israel will be as fruitful as the descendants of both young men (48:19).

The lesson for us in this scene is that God's plans and purposes aren't necessarily understandable to us. What may seem right and proper to us from our human perspective may not be that way at all in terms of God's eternal purposes. Sometimes God uses people who seem of little outward importance to be a blessing to those who appear to be greater. This was certainly true in the case of Joseph who came from prison and slavery to become the number two ruler in Egypt. Many years later Paul captured this whole idea when he wrote, "But God hath chosen the foolish things of the world to confound the wise; and God hath chosen the weak things of the world to confound the things which are mighty" (1 Cor. 1:27).

God Chooses Whom He Will

In 1987 a prominent news magazine chose Corazon Aquino to be its "Woman of the Year." The story of her rise to the office of president of the Philippines from her place as a widowed housewife just the year before, defies the understanding of everyone who professes to know how the world works. Her selection as president over a powerful dictator in a rigged election is a vivid twentieth-century testimony not to the way the world works, but to the way God acts. During the election Marcos had claimed that God's blessing was rightfully his. "God is with us!" he said. "God knows that to protect the Filipino people we must win."

But Cory Aquino knew that she would win not because of her own power but because of God's power. It was in a quiet prayer retreat that she became assured God was calling her to a place of leadership. Then when God blessed her with victory, she didn't gloat and say, "I have won." Instead she said quietly, "The long agony is over." God chooses whom He pleases, not to exalt one person over another but so His purposes will be fulfilled according to plan.

This is the assurance that Jacob—Israel—gives Joseph now. He can be certain that God's purposes will be done, and "God shall be with you, and bring you again unto the land of your fathers" (48:21). In addition, we read that Jacob allotted Joseph two portions of the promised land, to be named for his two sons, while all the other brothers received just one portion. This is why there was no tribe of Israel named for Joseph.

Other translations refer to the second portion or extra portion as "one mountaintop" or "one ridge" of land more than your brothers. Some Bible students believe this is a direct reference to the city of Shechem in the Palestinian hill country that Jacob took from the Amorites with sword and bow (48:22).

Historically, the promise Jacob made to Joseph on his deathbed was fulfilled. Ephraim did indeed become the strongest tribe especially during the early days of Israel's national life. The prophet Hosea refers to Ephraim not just as the name of one tribe but as the representative of the entire Northern Kingdom (Hosea 5:3). And as for Joseph's "extra portion" or "ridge," we read later in the book of Joshua that it was at Shechem where Joseph's bones were laid in their final resting place (Joshua 24:32). Centuries later it would be near Shechem that Jesus revealed His identity to the Samaritan woman at Jacob's well (John 4:5–26).

Jacob Calls His Sons Together

Jacob's final act is to call all of his sons together around his bedside to hear his last words for them, "that I may tell you that which shall befall you in the last days. Gather yourselves together, and hear, ye sons of Jacob; and hearken unto Israel your father" (49:1–2).

Deathbed words were very important to people in the ancient Near East. They were believed to be divinely inspired. In the same way a blessing, or a curse, released a power that made a difference. Much later a pagan ruler of Moab hired a diviner named Balaam to place a curse on Israel because he was convinced of Balaam's power, "I wot [know] that he whom thou blessest is blessed, and he whom thou cursest is cursed" (Num. 22:6). Jesus told His disciples, "Whatsoever ye shall bind on earth shall be bound in heaven, and whatsoever ye shall loose on earth shall be loosed in heaven" (Matt. 18:18).

There is an important lesson for us here. There is a power in the spoken word. And words that are once spoken can never be taken back again. Recently I heard a highly educated theologian address a group of college students on the nature of God. In the course of his lecture he used an unfortunate phrase, in which his audience understood him to say that God "regresses" when we do. Most of the audience were not trained theologians and everyone was very confused and disturbed by what the man was trying to say.

The Power of the Spoken Word

Later in the question-and-answer session, the speaker was asked to explain what he meant by the word *regress.* Instead of admitting that he had used the wrong word, he tried to modify and clarify what he had said, but that only led to more confusion and even anger on the part of the audience. After the session, the learned man was overheard to say to a friend, "I will never use that word again!"

Most of us have held our tongues when we should have spoken out, or wagged our tongues when we should have kept them still. In either case we have become a curse when we should have been a blessing. God's way is so often just the opposite. We see this in the dying words of Jesus on the cross. If there ever was a time when God might have laid His curse upon the whole human race, it was then. By all rights, Jesus' death should have become a curse on our character and destiny forever. But instead, Jesus became a blessing, as He said "Father, forgive them, for they know not what they do" (Luke 23:34). It is only by that kind of forgiving love that we can love those who curse us, and bless those who hate us.

Later in the lesson we will see that Joseph's brothers feared that their father's death would bring down Joseph's curse upon them, which they knew they deserved. Will Joseph turn on his brothers when their father is gone? We'll find the answer to that question shortly. But first we turn to Jacob's last words to his sons given to us in the form of poetry. He called each of his sons in turn to his deathbed (49:2), and his perceptions and predictions give us some insight into the fate of each of the twelve tribes of Israel up to the time of David. Each one has some application to our own lives, just as each one of Jacob's sons represents some character trait in each of us that could be either a blessing or a curse, depending upon how we live our lives.

Reuben's Lost Potential

Reuben, the firstborn, is described as a man of tremendous potential. Jacob refers to him as "my might" and the "first fruits of my strength." He has the potential of being the proudest and the most powerful of Jacob's sons (49:3). But after this glowing introduction, we are let down, because like the poem, Reuben starts gloriously and never lives up to his potential.

Jacob describes Reuben as "unstable as water" (49:4). The word *unstable* is a translation of a Hebrew word used to describe a lawless mob as "vain and light persons" in Judges 9:4. The word is also used in describing the false prophets as "light and treacherous persons" in Zephaniah 3:4.

It isn't that Reuben is weak, but he is wild, undisciplined, and impulsive, like his Uncle Esau was in his early years. Reuben can be compared to an unrestrained flood that overflows its banks. He does not stay within the bounds of moral discipline because he cannot control his covetous desires. Specifically, Jacob accuses him of defiling his father's bed by sleeping with Bilhah, Jacob's concubine (35:22).

This judgment on Reuben's impulsive behavior and moral weakness is reflected in the later history of the tribe of Reuben both during the wilderness years with Moses and after the conquest of Canaan. In the wilderness the descendants of Reuben rebelled against Moses' leadership (Num. 16:1). After the conquest of Canaan by the twelve tribes, Reuben's tribe settled in the territory that lay east of the Dead Sea. Although powerful for a time, their effectiveness was later diminished by poor leadership and social instability.

God has given all of us great potential. I once heard a preacher describe each person in his congregation as an "explosive possibility." By this he meant that God has invested in each person the possibility of making a great impact on the people around them—not through spectacular exploits but through the development of the fruit of His Spirit in us: patience, joy, love, mercy, and forgiveness (see Gal. 5:22–23).

Jacob speaks of Reuben as having the excellency of dignity and power (49:3). But, tragically, Reuben wasted his God-given dignity in having sexual relations with a woman who wasn't his wife. He had also been guilty of misusing his God-given power in a brutal act of vengeance against a whole city for the crime of just one of its citizens.

Whenever our dignity and power are sold out in impulsive, lustful, or vengeful actions, their God-given potential for good is lost completely. Paul said it best when he wrote, "But earnestly desire the higher gifts. And I will show you a still more excellent way" (1 Cor. 12:31 RSV).

Next Jacob turns his attention to Simeon and Levi, the second and third sons of Leah. In so many words he labels them as men who are vicious and violent (49:5–6). Again, this may refer to the ruthless slaughter of the people of Shechem (34:25–31). Both of these sons had incurred Jacob's displeasure and lost his favor.

A look into the future tells us that these two vengeful brothers suffered less than noble fates. Centuries later in Canaan the tribe of Simeon was scattered and eventually absorbed partly by the tribe of Judah (Josh. 19:2–9) and partly by the northern tribes (2 Chron. 34:6). Their distinct identity was lost. On the other hand, because of their service to the Lord (Exod. 32:25–29; Num. 18:20–23), the name

Simeon and Levi: Sons of Wrath

of Levi was cleared, but the Levites did not receive an inheritance of land, only certain cities were designated for them among the other tribes (Josh. 14:1–3; 21:1–42). In all of this we see that Jacob's prophecy was fulfilled.

Jacob condemned these two sons of his for their uncontrolled anger and aggression. Anger can serve a useful purpose when it is used to defend the innocent rather than destroy them. But when anger is used to defend our pride by hurting others, it becomes an "instrument of cruelty" or a weapon of violence (49:5).

The Apostle Paul echoed this theme when he wrote, "But now ye also put off all these; anger, wrath, malice" (Col. 3:8). And in another place he wrote, "Let all bitterness, and wrath, and anger, and clamour, and evil speaking, be put away from you, with all malice (Eph. 4:31).

Will Rogers, the great American humorist of a past generation, used to say, "People who fly into a rage always make a bad landing." Simeon and Levi "made a bad landing" and lost their father's blessing because of their vicious tempers. In God's providence one son lost his identity completely while the other eventually gained a new identity through faithful service.

Judah, Lion of the Kingdom

As Jacob considers his sons according to their ages, he turns his attention to Judah, Leah's fourth son (49:8–12). In Jacob's vision of the future, the tribe of Judah is destined for conquest and kingship (49:8, 10). Judah was the one who would be praised by his brethren—the word "praise" used here is really a play on Judah's name (29:35).

In the pictorial language of these verses we see the future prominence of the tribe of Judah. It was from the tribe of Judah that David came during the Golden Age of Israel's history when the kingdom was united under one king. Many centuries after David's time it was the tribe of Judah that formed Jesus' earthly heritage. And it was in Jesus, the risen Christ—the "Lion of the tribe of Judah" (Rev. 5:5)—that God's people of all time have received the promise of the true riches of God's grace. Jacob's ancient blessing given to his son Judah has become a blessing for us as well.

Zebulun, Prisoner of the Sea

Jacob disposes with Zebulun, Leah's fifth son, with just a few words. We're told that this tribe would live along the sea and its territory would border on Zidon (49:13)—present-day Sidon in Lebanon. Both the coastland of Israel and the port of Sidon were not conquered under Joshua's campaign. Those areas were ruled by pagan Philistines and Phoenicians.

There is strong indication that the tribe of Zebulun, along with Asher and Gad provided forced labor at times for the pagan city of Sidon (Judg. 5:17–18). But whether forcibly or voluntarily, Zebulun's descendants apparently lived in rather close collaboration with the pagan Sea People who lived along the coast. And all of this seems to tie in closely with the Hebrew word for Zebulun which means "to dwell with."

Perhaps the best lesson we learn from this son of Jacob is that there is great risk in living with and being intimately involved with unbelievers. To associate closely with people who have no interest whatever in God and in the highest moral and spiritual values is to risk becoming tainted ourselves. There's a great deal of truth in the old Chinese proverb, "He who lies down with dogs, soon comes up with fleas." Instead of careless association with unbelievers, it is much better to be able to say with the Psalmist, "Lord, thou hast been our dwellingplace in all generations" (Psa. 90:1).

Issachar: Son of Burden

This son of Leah is pictured by his father here as a carrier of burdens who "became a servant unto tribute"—one who was a victim of forced labor (49:14–15). The implication seems to be that Issachar may have seriously overextended himself because he loved ease and pleasant circumstances. He eventually became enslaved.

If that is the case, a modern counterpart of Issachar might be the person who foolishly uses his plastic credit cards until he carries a double burden of debt that has him enslaved by his creditors. A preoccupation with material gain has brought defeat to many otherwise good people.

Dan: the Son of Harsh Judgment

Jacob has just a few words for Dan, whose name in Hebrew means "judge" or a person who dispenses justice (49:16–18). The background on Dan is meager, but it seems that even though he was a man with great potential, he used his power of judgment for spite and treachery. He is compared to a snake that hides out in the brush by the roadside and then strikes out at unsuspecting passersby.

In later centuries when Israel moved in to occupy the Promised Land, the tribe of Dan was assigned territory along part of the west coast between the area allotted to Judah and Ephraim. It was a small area dominated by the Philistines whom they never completely conquered. Instead of exercising good judgment they seemed to be masters of bad judgment, even to the point of sending an expedition to the northernmost part of Canaan in an attempt to settle where they weren't supposed to. Good judgment is a blessing; bad judgment is a curse.

How careful we as Christians need to be in how we use our capacity for judgment. We can use it for good or for backbiting, as in the case of Dan.

Paul gave us wise words when he wrote, "Let us not therefore judge one another any more: but judge this rather, that no man put a stumblingblock or an occasion to fall in his brother's way" (Rom. 14:13). Our task as Christians is not to tear one another down but to build each other up in the faith of Jesus Christ.

Gad: the Strong Defender

Jacob has little to say to this seventh son of his, but he is praised for being an overcomer in the end (49:19). The land allotted to Gad's descendants when the Hebrews occupied Canaan was east of the Jordan River, between the area given to Reuben and Manasseh.

Later in the Book of Judges the people of Gad are praised for the way they prevailed over their enemies and occupied their territory (Judg. 11). Theirs was not an easy life, but as Jacob had predicted many years before, they were overcomers.

These two brothers and their descendants are pictured by the old Patriarch as receivers of rich blessings (49:20–21). At the time of the occupation of Canaan, Asher's land lay on the coastal strip between Mount Carmel and Phoenicia to the north. It was fertile land—described as producing "royal dainties," delicacies or pleasures suitable for a king. Under the circumstances it was quite fitting that the root meaning of Asher's name is "happy."

Naphtali, whose name means "wrestling," was also favored by his father's last words. He is compared to a deer that has been held captive and then released. At the time of Canaan's occupation his descendants were allotted extremely rich land along the northeastern border. During the time of Christ the land of Naphtali was a part of Galilee.

Throughout its history, the tribe of Naphtali remained strong and vigorous in its defense of the country.

Asher and Naphtali: Heirs of Joy and Freedom

As might be expected, Jacob is lavish in his comments and blessing for Joseph (49:22–26). In picturesque language he describes Joseph as a "fruitful bough," fed by a spring, a real blessing in a dry country such as Palestine. He speaks of Joseph's suffering and time of trial, and then refers to Joseph's triumph with God's help.

As we read Jacob's choice of words in his message to Joseph, we sense his great feeling of love and respect. He pays proper homage to this son of his who was set apart from his brothers to fulfill God's marvelous plan for His people.

You will recall that in Joseph's earlier meeting with his father, his two sons Ephraim and Manasseh were promised a double inheritance of land. At the time of the occupation of Canaan the land allotted Ephraim and Manasseh was located in the central part of the country.

But once again we see that a great potential isn't always realized. Ephraim would fail God because of

Joseph: Son of Promise

pride (Judg. 12:1; Isa. 28:1–3) and idolatry (Hos. 4:17). The people of Manasseh would later join with Ephraim in fighting against the Southern kingdom of Judah for the kingly line. Both tribes were guilty of wickedness and greediness (Isa. 9:20–21). Once again, we see that those who are most favored are not always the most faithful.

Benjamin: a Mixed Blessing

Jacob comes now to his youngest son (49:27). Benjamin's name means "son of my right hand." But his words come as a bit of surprise as he refers to Benjamin as a ravening wolf who hunts and kills by day and divides up the spoil in the evening. Many years later Moses pronounced a more positive blessing on Benjamin's descendants: "The beloved of the Lord shall dwell in safety by him; and the Lord shall cover him all the day long, and he shall dwell between his shoulders" (Deut. 33:12).

Both Jacob and Moses tell some of the truth about the tribe of Benjamin. These were fierce and spirited fighters (Judg. 19–21). Because of the decimation of the tribe in the settlement process, they became the smallest of the tribes, but were always leaders (Psa. 68:27).

The land allotted Benjamin in Canaan was a rectangle some twenty-six miles long by twelve miles wide and included what later became the city of Jerusalem.

Jacob's Last Request and His Death

The last of Jacob's dying statements to his sons, which the Genesis writer has carefully preserved for us, is specific instructions for his burial (49:29–32). He is to be taken back to Hebron and buried with his father and grandfather, Isaac and Abraham, in the cave that had been purchased many years before from Ephron the Hittite (49:29). When his instructions were completed, the aged Patriarch lay back on his bed and died (49:33).

A Time of Mourning and Jacob's Burial

Jacob's death is followed by a time of mourning for the family. Joseph ordered Jacob's body to be embalmed (50:1–2), though this was not a Hebrew custom. But he was thinking ahead. When the period of mourning was over, Joseph approached Pharaoh to request permission to leave the court, because he had promised his father on his deathbed that his body would be returned to Canaan for burial.

Pharaoh granted permission for Jacob's body to be escorted from Egypt to Hebron in southern Canaan. We're told that all of Jacob's family made the trip and that they were escorted by a cortege of Egyptian officials in chariots and on horses—"a very great company" (50:7–9).

We can be quite sure that when this impressive caravan entered Canaan, it attracted a great deal of attention. We're told the procession stopped at a place described as the threshing floor of Atad. We don't know where that was, but we are told they progressed on to Hebron and buried Jacob "in the cave of the field of Machpelah, which Abraham bought with the field for a possession of a burying-place of Ephron the Hittite, before Mamre" (50:13).

Jacob had once more come home—to the land of his fathers. His had been a long pilgrimage. In Jacob we have a marvelous example of transformation, and a vivid picture of the grace of God at work in a very human person. On the banks of the River Jabbok, Jacob, a cheater and deceiver, became Israel, a man of God. What God did for Jacob, He can and will do for you and me.

Joseph Returns to Egypt

Before leaving Egypt Joseph had given Pharaoh his solemn promise that as soon as their father was buried, he and his brothers would return. So we read now that "Joseph returned into Egypt, he, and his brethren, and all that went up with him" (50:14). In many ways, this must have been difficult after having a short glimpse of their homeland, but Joseph had to resume the work to which God had called him.

Joseph's Brothers Fear Revenge

With their father dead and buried, the brothers now felt that Joseph would have his revenge. There was just no way they could imagine that he could so easily forgive them for the crimes they had committed against him many years before. Now, they believed, with the restraint of their father's presence removed, Joseph's wrath would thunder in on them.

So they sent him a message supposedly drafted by their father before he died: "Forgive, I pray thee now, the trespass of thy brethren, and their sin; for they did unto thee evil" (50:17). We are then told that when this message reached Joseph, he cried. Imagine, if you can, the sorrow and frustration he must have felt when he realized fully that his brothers still didn't seem to understand God's role in all that had happened.

The First Pillar of Faith

Joseph's fears and concerns were verified when his brothers "fell down before his face; and they said, Behold, we be thy servants [slaves]" (50:18). Again, his early dream is being fulfilled, but Joseph has learned to transform fury into faith, and his answer to his brothers sums up the message God has for us, I believe, in this part of the lesson. Each part of Joseph's answer reveals a pillar of the biblical faith we have inherited.

First, Joseph asks, "Am I in the place of God?" (50:19). The Bible instructs us to leave judgment to God. The Apostle Paul spoke very clearly about this, "Dearly beloved, avenge not yourselves, but rather give place unto wrath [leave that up to God]: for it is written, Vengeance is mine; I will repay, saith the Lord" (Rom. 12:19).

Joseph's question, "Am I in the place of God?" is just as relevant now as it was thirty-five hundred years ago. We are all threatened by the temptation to play God when it comes to setting spiritual standards for other people. We want to decide on right interpretations and right actions and then judge another's spirituality by our standards. How foolish and how tragic! When we're tempted to judge and condemn our fellow Christians, we will do well to ask ourselves, "Am I in the place of God?"

The Second Pillar of Faith

The second pillar of our biblical faith is found in these next words of Joseph: "But as for you, ye thought evil against me; but God meant it unto good" (50:20). These are powerful words of reassurance and in many ways are the key to understanding the biblical message of faith. God alone is in control. He alone can take the evil that we do or that is done to us and direct it toward the fulfillment of His plans and purposes.

The fulfillment of God's plan for the world and for us is not dependent on our success or failure. His will *will be done* on earth even as it is done in heaven. We have a marvelous example of this in the Gospels. Jesus' betrayal in the Garden of Gethsemane, His arrest, trial, and crucifixion, all portray the massive attempt of evil to defeat God's plan of salvation. But the last word came in the Resurrection as God turned evil into triumph.

The Third Pillar of Faith

In repaying evil with good, Joseph reassures his brothers, "Now therefore fear ye not: I will nourish you, and your little ones." The writer adds, "And he comforted them, and spake kindly unto them" (50:21). Here Joseph models a marvelous example of forgiving love. It wasn't a love that the brothers deserved any more than we deserve the unmerited favor of God in Christ.

The great comedian Jack Benny was once presented with an award honoring all of his years on the stage, radio, and television. Overcome with emotion Benny held the award in silence for a few moments, and then he said, "You know, I really don't deserve this award. But I'm nearsighted, and I don't deserve that either."

Mr. Benny was right. We may not always deserve many of the difficult things that happen to us, and we certainly don't deserve all of the good that happens. Joseph's life is a clear testimony of that truth today, even as it has been across the centuries. God's love, His grace, and His truth are indeed eternal.

Joseph Dies in God's Promise

Now the Genesis story comes to an end as we read that Joseph lived 110 years and died in Egypt (50:22), an honored man, surrounded by his family, and upheld by his God to the very end. The Genesis writer tells us that Joseph lived to see his children's children and to pass on to them the blessing of his fathers (50:23).

As Joseph was dying he assured his family that ultimately God would guide them back to the Land of Promise according to His covenant with Abraham, Isaac, and Jacob (50:24). Then before breathing his last Joseph exacted a promise from his family that when they did leave Egypt, they would take his bones with them for final burial. Finally, we read that Joseph died, his body was embalmed, and placed in "a coffin in Egypt"—that is, a temporary grave (50:25–26).

A Story for All Time

The Book of Genesis ends by pointing to a hope beyond the immediate circumstances. We know that Joseph's grave was indeed temporary, for several hundred years later Moses saw to it that Joseph's bones were with the Israelites when they left Egypt (Exod. 13:19). And when the Israelites finally moved into Canaan, the writer of Joshua tells us, "And the bones of Joseph, which the children of Israel brought up out of Egypt, buried they in Shechem, in a parcel of ground which Jacob bought of the sons of Hamor the father of Shechem for an hundred pieces of silver: and it became the inheritance of the children of Joseph" (Josh. 24:32).

Joseph had finally come home to the Land of Promise. And then all of the descendants of Jacob were free to occupy the land in obedience to God's instructions. Now, over three thousand years later, we share in that promise through our freedom in Jesus Christ.

I will never forget the words of Dr. Martin Luther King, Jr., when he gathered an oppressed people in front of the Lincoln Memorial in Washington in 1963. He, like Joseph, had a dream—not a dream of personal glory but of freedom. On that memorable day Dr. King spoke of the kind of freedom that offers love in place of revenge and genesis instead of genocide. Then Dr. King closed his speech with the hope that the Book of Genesis points to—from the first moments of creation to the last days of Joseph, "Free at last! Free at last! Thank God Almighty, we are free at last!"

Father, The source of my hope lies beyond my circumstances, disabilities, restrictions, or other things that might hem me in. You are my hope and my salvation. AMEN.

WHAT THIS SCRIPTURE MEANS TO ME
Genesis 47:27—50:26

During a recent church-sponsored retreat, I watched the television movie "The Doll Maker" for the third time. The lead character in this powerful and moving film is a woman named Gerte, the mother of a large family who lived in the hills of Kentucky.

In 1944, the entire family moved to Detroit to join the father, who was working in an automobile factory. Gerte felt stifled by her noisy and cramped surroundings, and had difficulty adjusting to the city life-style. Her accent and customs were not accepted by most of the people around her. Throughout the movie, Gerte was faced with problems and crises which demanded strength, courage, and faith. But the personal qualities which sustained and inspired her through this whole ordeal were her desire and determination to return "home."

Following the viewing of this film, we discussed our impressions and voiced comments, likes, dislikes, and questions which the movie raised. Eventually, our discussion centered around the question, "Where is home?"

Based on Gerte's experience, this question was easily answered. Home for her was in Kentucky—the place where she was born and raised. Her parents, siblings, aunts, uncles, and cousins all lived a relatively short distance from one another.

But many of the participants in this retreat had entirely different backgrounds and experiences. We heard comments such as: "My father is in the Air Force, so my family moves every two to three years"; "My parents moved to a different state after thirty years in the same house. It doesn't seem like home to me"; and "My parents divorced after I left for college. Where is home for me?"

Today we live in a fast-paced and mobile society. Our jobs, interests, and places of residence change more frequently and rapidly than ever before. We no longer seem to have the security of a lifelong "home."

In this lesson, Jacob made a dying request to Joseph, "If now I have found grace [favor] in thy sight . . . deal kindly and truly with me; bury me not, I pray thee, in Egypt. But let me lie with my fathers . . . bury me in their burying place" (Gen. 47:29, 30).

Jacob did not want to be buried in Egypt because he had gained his identity as a man of faith in the land of his fathers, Abraham and Isaac. It was in the land of Canaan where God had revealed Himself to Jacob in a dream (Gen. 28:10–15), and where he wished to return to be with his ancestors who shared his faith as his spiritual fathers.

As we journey through life, our physical homes may change. It may be impossible or impractical for us to return to the place of our birth when we die. That is why I think it is important to view life as a spiritual journey, one which will eventually lead to our spiritual home. And by establishing and maintaining a personal relationship with God, our spiritual Father, we can gain confidence and assurance from His promise of eternal life for those who believe in Him.

Our occupations, avocations, and vocations may lead us to many different towns, cities, and countries of the world. There may be times when we become homesick for the scenery, people, and places that were once familiar to us. But instead of focusing our attention on the past and what we have left behind, we need to look ahead to the One who can guide us through the present and lead us to our future Home.